God 101

Jewish Ideals, Beliefs,
and Practices for
Renewing Your Faith

Rabbi Terry A. Bookman

A Perigee Book

A Perigee Book
Published by The Berkley Publishing Group
A division of Penguin Putnam Inc.
375 Hudson Street
New York, New York 10014

Copyright © 2000 by Terry A. Bookman
Book design by Tiffany Kukec
Cover design by Dorothy Wachtenheim
Cover art adapted from a painting by Lucille Colin

First edition: March 2001

Published simultaneously in Canada.

The Penguin Putnam Inc. World Wide Web site address is
http://www.penguinputnam.com

Library of Congress Cataloging-in-Publication Data

Bookman, Terry.
   God 101 : Jewish ideals, beliefs, and practices for renewing your faith / Terry
A. Bookman.
    p. cm.
   ISBN 0-399-52658-7
   1. Jewish way of life. 2. God (Judaism) 3. Spiritual life—Judaism.
I. Title: God one-oh-one. II. Title.

BM723.B62 2001
296.3'11—dc21   00-062408

Printed in the United States of America

10 9 8 7 6 5 4 3 2 1

Dedicated to the memory of Bubby Esther and Grandpa Max Bernfeld, who taught me about God without my even knowing it. Their personal example continues as a shining presence in my life.

Contents

Acknowledgments

I want to begin by thanking John Duff and Perigee for asking me to write this book. Their commitment to producing quality books on human spirituality is truly a gift and an inspiration.

When I make changes in my students' papers, they want to know why I "corrected" them. I reply that I am merely "editing" what they wrote, so that their work more clearly states what they wanted to say in the first place. I want to thank Jennifer Repo for being my editor on this book. If it communicates to you, thank her as well. Kara Moskowitz, her assistant, also read this manuscript, and her suggestions and insights were most helpful.

To my agent, Julie Merberg, of Roundtable Press, I am fully aware that I have become an author only with your help, encouragement, and guidance. You believed in me and what I have to say before anyone else did. I am forever grateful. I look forward to a lifetime of working with you and to being a part of your life as well.

The "other woman" in my life is my assistant, Claudia Goodman. I want to thank her for making my very complicated life work, and for all her help in the tedious task of manuscript production. She too, is a blessing.

The original push for this book came from my friend Joy Ness, who challenges me each day to answer her questions. She convinced me that this book is needed, and she has always believed in its ultimate success. Her enthusiasm for this project carried me through the toughest days.

No words would ever be enough to thank my life partner, Karen Sobel, and our children—Ariel, Jonah, Micah, and Jesse— for their support, understanding, and sacrifices. Though they appear by name from time to time in this book, know that they are a part of every word I write, every breath I take.

My synagogue, Temple Beth Am in Miami, is an amazing place because the people who call it their "home away from home" are devoted to making it so. Their embrace of me and my work is a dream come true. I thank them for allowing me the space to share myself and my words with all of you.

Every page of this book is the result of those courageous souls who shared their struggles, hopes, questions, and dreams in our God classes and workshops for these past ten years. I only pray that in some small measure our journeying together helped you discover and renew your relationship with the Holy One of All Life.

Ever since I can remember, my life has been intertwined with God. I thank Her for Her embrace; I thank Him for His faith in me. I am more than blessed. May I always be worthy of this trust.

God 101

Part One

Questions We Ask

Introduction

God Makes a Comeback

I get a call from my brother one afternoon.

"You're finally in!" I hear him say.

"What did I do?"

"Did you see the latest issue of *U.S. News and World Report?* There's this big article about God. You're in, bro. I can't believe it. After all these years, you are actually popular."

That was my brother's idea of a compliment. Anyway, I had not seen it, but I went out and bought it. My brother, Robert, was referring to the April 4, 1994, issue, which explored recent trends in America among educated people who were searching for God by both conventional and unconventional means. The article stated that "the United States [is] the most religious of the Western democracies. In fact, the United States appears to be more religious today that it was at its founding." *U.S. News and World Report* was not alone in its conclusions. Many of the other leading national magazines and journals—including *Time, Newsweek,* and *Psychology Today*—reported similar findings.

Though in the nineteenth century the philosopher Friedrich

Nietzsche declared, "God is dead!" by the end of the twentieth century God might very well have responded, "Reports of my demise are greatly exaggerated." Indeed, in all kinds of circles, God is making a comeback. God talk, once reserved for theologians and seminarians, has made its way to the university, the workplace, the gym, and the kitchen table. Once again, issues of faith are acceptable conversation.

The origins of God's marginalization in modernity began with the Enlightenment in Western Europe. Ushered in by Napoleon and the French Revolution toward the end of the eighteenth century, the Enlightenment brought much good. Though originally limited only to white men, democracy, freedom, individual citizenship, and universal education were just some of the gifts later realized in modernity.

But these gifts came at a great price, especially for Jewish and other religious communities. In Germany, and then later in France, the ghetto walls came tumbling down. Jews, once isolated and kept apart, gained access and acceptance in all quarters of European society. The synagogue (and the church as well) were replaced by the university as the central address of "modern man." The university became the site of rational discourse, of science, of progress, and in such a place, God was not a welcome guest. God and religion were viewed as obsolete creations of the Dark Ages, as pariahs that held us back, preventing us from realizing our full human and societal potential. Religious communities rushed to prove that they, too, were modern, universal in outlook, repositories of ethical conduct. They eschewed their particularism, their rituals, stories of miracles, and anything that smacked of mystical or a-rational thinking. Worship services included long sermons that sounded like college lectures, minimizing prayer and any sense of a personal God who could intervene in the lives of people.

It is easy for us to look back at what these religious communities did and accuse them of not being "spiritual" or engaging.

But that would be an oversimplification. It was an age of reason and great optimism for a world that seemed on the brink of the much-hoped-for universal "brotherhood of man" and world peace. For them, the path to that world lay in our rational faculties, that which united us. As we became more secular, as we shifted from a God-centered to a human-centered worldview, the anthropomorphic way of talking about God seemed old-fashioned, out-of-date. God, if talked about at all, became an "idea," a "force within human beings and nature," a "power," even "the highest ideal"—rational, scientific terms. God was marginalized, becoming less of an everyday reality in people's lives.

For the Jewish community in particular, becoming "less religious" (but not less Jewish) seemed a small price to pay for admission into the general society. While paying lip service to a "belief in God," Jews let go of the religion that separated them from their fellow citizens, declaring that one could be a Jew in the home but a mensch or "person" in the streets. They stopped overt expressions of religious behavior, especially in the realm of ritual, calendar, and dress. Shabbat became "Saturday," a menu was an opportunity to eat foods long forbidden by dietary laws, and one wore the clothes dictated by fashion.

Jews also formed secular organizations that allowed them to socialize with one another and do good works in the community together with other Jews. This was the beginning of the organizations that would come to dominate Jewish life in modernity— the American Jewish Committee and Congress, B'nai B'rith International, the Federations of Jewish Philanthropy, the YM/WHA and the Jewish Community Centers, Zionist groups like Hadassah and the Jewish National Fund supporting the return to Palestine, even Jewish country clubs and Jewish hospitals. All were attempts to keep Jews Jewish and in contact with other Jews *without God.* While synagogue life never totally disappeared, it became child- and event-oriented at best, trivialized at worst. Synagogue was one of those "affiliations" that proper people had to have. And so synagogues were built to educate children (at least to the age of bar mitzvah) and allow Jews to take their place in the modern world, but not to have any real impact on adults or the serious life choices they made each day.

By the end of the twentieth century, however, all this had changed. Two world wars, the Great Depression, the Holocaust, the Cold War, the ongoing brutalities and human rights violations in almost every corner of the globe, the Korean War, the Vietnam War, the breakdown of traditional family and community, cynical regard for institutions and our leaders, a growing relativism that told us "What is right for me may not be right for you" to the point that we have come to question whether or not there are any absolutes—all of these events and developments—have had a negative impact on our trust and faith in modernity's ability to solve our ills. In fact, given the banality of modern life, its materialism and its trendy fadism, its Me-ism and selfishness, its empty promises to make our lives easier even as they become more difficult and confusing, we have begun a search for "something more," something eternal and bigger than ourselves, something that can ground us and give us lasting meaning, something that can truly fill us up and dispel the emptiness we feel. That gnawing doubt about our lives has led, I believe, to a search for ultimate truth. Such a search inevitably will lead us to explore very seriously the faith claims of our religious traditions and to open ourselves to the possibility that God is real— and has been real all along. Couple that with a resurgence in ethnic pride and a pluralism that celebrates diversity rather than eliminating it—the salad bowl as opposed to the melting pot— and we see the cultural forces that have shaped our new reality.

And so, the God courses and workshops I offered fifteen years ago to a handful of searchers are now filled on the first day of registration; books on religion and spirituality are a major portion of publication markets; articles on religious topics in major magazines are rather commonplace; films and television programs deal thoughtfully with God, afterlife, angels; religious and Jewish studies departments have sprouted up at hundreds of universities; sophisticated Hollywood stars speak openly about their spiritual search and longings; rabbis teach classes in every major downtown business area; and, perhaps to your own surprise, you are reading this book.

Where will all this lead? I am not sure. I hope that the result will not be full-scale rejection of modernity, as we have seen in some fundamentalist movements around the world. While we all have friends and family members who call themselves *"ba'alei t'shuvah,"* the Jewish version of "born again," returning to self-imposed, cloistered (sociological if not actually physical) ghettos, that is not a promising option for most of us. Those of us who have been educated to think for ourselves and to do so critically would like to keep at least one foot firmly planted in the modern world, for it has brought us much that is good and worthwhile.

But we want more than that. We want a faith that will allow us to be ourselves and not require that we reject our lifestyles. We want to know that our lives are worthwhile, make sense, really matter. We would like reassurance that we are not "bad people," even though we have strayed from our ancestral faith and tradition. Many have been "spiritually wounded" by the negative experiences they had in synagogue when they were growing up; they need to be shown a way back so that they can heal. That way must grant us full gender equality, the opportunity to explore the limits of our human potential in any field of endeavor, and the personal autonomy that allows us the exercise of conscience. We are open to a faith that can be a-rational but not irrational, and community that is nurturing and supportive without being stifling. Having sensed the possibilities of a holistic approach to living, we are unwilling to bifurcate our lives. We insist on keen intellectual honesty and an openness to truth, no matter the source. We are tired of religion that is somber, childish chauvinistic, or shallow; we want to be challenged and uplifted, to feel the joy and celebration of faith and tradition, to be guided on a path that can speak to us each and every day. We want to be engaged with the society in which we live, repairing its brokenness, healing its pain. And we will no longer tolerate religious leaders who want to crush our egos or control our lives, who insist that we "break with our past," our families, our friends. Instead, we want to be accepted for who we are and where we are, without the hidden agenda of where they want us to be.

This is not the latest Yuppie version of wanting it all. It is about finding a God with whom we can be in a mature, adult relationship, and a faith tradition that treats us like the capable, intelligent human beings we truly are. It is about finding meaning and community, and our place in this vast universe that embraces us, anchors us, and sets us truly free.

God is, indeed, making a comeback. We welcome the Holy One back into our communities and into our lives. We know we will have to make some room, some accommodations for God to enter. With both trepidation and excitement, we ready ourselves to begin that quest and that challenge. *Bah-rooch Ah-tah Ah-doe-nigh*/Beloved are You, Adonai, each and every day, for the challenges You set before us, for the opportunities to serve, for the blessings You bestow upon us openly and in secret, for the miracles of life that surround us on all sides, for Your guidance and Your presence with us on our journey through life.

Question 1

Is There Really (a) God?

Did God create us, or did we create God? There are really only two possibilities. Either we created God or God created us. Oh, we could play the agnostic game and say "maybe." Though I suppose that choice could be intellectually honest for some of you reading these words, my kids know that when I say "maybe," it really means "no," but I want their mother to be the one to say it, or I am just buying time, hoping they will forget about their request. Just as I eventually have to answer their questions, we will have to answer this one sooner or later. But when it comes to this question, we answer it with the way we live our lives.

There was this couple in a class I was teaching. I had asked if anyone ever felt close to God—not believed in or had knowledge of, but simply felt close. The husband raised his hand and said in a loud and excited voice, "We just came back from a ski trip. I was coming down the slope when suddenly I hit a whiteout . . . couldn't see a thing. I could have waited there, but sometimes these things take hours, and it was really cold. Then and there I decided to point my skis down the slope and go for it. I knew God was with me and would not allow anything bad to happen. And sure enough, I skied down without a problem." As he finished, with a big smile on his face, the entire class started staring at his wife, waiting for her response. "Blind luck!" she said. "The man is just plain lucky!" Two possibilities—God or luck.

The statement that there is a God is a statement of faith. It is not a statement of fact. There is no proof of God. None. However, the statement that there is no God is also a statement of faith. It, too, is not a statement of fact. Neither belief can be proved or disproved. I can point to reasons why I have faith that there is a God—cogent reasons as far as I am concerned—but they are not a proof of anything. An atheist can also point to cogent reasons. They, too, are not proof. We all have faith in something. Atheists place their faith in humanity, or in the creations of people—political systems, government, society, law, movements for the betterment of humanity, and so on. The best we can do is stake a claim and live our lives accordingly.

Nevertheless, there have been, throughout the ages, attempts to prove God's existence. Today, it is done with computers, a modern *gammatria*/number interpretation checking every 176th or 423rd letter in the Bible to spell out some secret message encoded in the text. It kind of reminds me of playing the song "Strawberry Fields Forever" backward to find out that Paul McCartney was dead. Proof for the existence of God is not new because doubting God's reality is also not new. We are not the first generation of doubters. And when those Russian cosmonauts went up in space in the early sixties and declared that they could not see God anywhere, they were not the first skeptics to call into question the physical reality of God in the world.

One of my favorite arguments for the proof of God comes from the rabbinic commentator and philospher Saadia Gaon in the Middle Ages. If one were to walk into a dining room and find a perfectly set table, plates all lined up, silverware on the proper side, water glasses and wine goblets where they ought to be, one could say all the place settings flew out of their cabinets and landed exactly where they belonged. It could have happened that way. But a rational person would assume that someone was responsible for setting that table. In like manner, when we consider that our world, the human body, the animal kingdom are so intricately structured, it is difficult to believe, it defies rationality, that it is all the result of random atoms colliding billions of years ago. I mean, it could all be the result of some cosmic accident, but when I look out my window now that I am living in Miami and I see what could be the very same bird that years ago was setting off to fly south for the winter, I recognize how orderly, how precise our world truly is, how everything fits together and has its place. For me, this is evidence enough that there is a greater intelligence operating in the universe, one that was responsible for setting up our world. I call that intelligence God. It is one way I have for relating to the Transcendent.

But just as we cannot prove God's reality, neither can we disprove it. Maybe that is why we speak of "faith." Faith is a kind of knowing that does not rely on rational or scientific proofs. Like intuition, or knowing that someone loves you, or the knowledge that derives from personal experience. When I say, "My experience teaches me that," I am stating something that I believe to be true, even if I cannot prove it. Faith is a way of knowing that is neither rational nor irrational. I believe that, in our postmodern world, we are becoming more and more open to other ways of knowing, ways that are not limited to the rational and the scientific, as important as they are for some things.

So, since we cannot prove our answer to the question of God's existence, we have to wager. We stake a claim. Many options call out to us, each claiming to be true. Our decision will not be so simple. If it were, I would not have had to write this book nor would you be reading it. The cynic states that God is a societal invention, created by leaders in order to control people and keep them in line. Freud understood God as a creation of the psyche, the father figure whom we project into the heavens, always ready to reward us when we do his bidding or to punish us when we disobey his rules. Marx said that God is the opiate of the masses, drugging us, the proletariat, so that we do not rise up in rebellion against the oppressive ruling class. Nietzsche and others declared that God is dead, that all we have is ourselves, and it really does not matter what we choose. All of these "truths" have attracted millions of adherents in modernity, with varying results. Each, I think, has its basis in humanity and thus shifts control and responsibility away from God and toward the human community. Each is idealistic in its own way, believing in the "perfectibility of man." And that, too, takes a great deal of faith.

A somewhat different slant, proposed by many modern psychotherapists and sociologists of religion and endorsed by a growing number of physicians, suggests that while God is indeed a human creation, faith serves a very beneficial purpose as the basis for healthy values, as a comfort in times of grief and sorrow, and as a source of unconditional love. Some recent studies even say that those who pray or meditate are healthier, even live longer. In other words, God is a good thing for people, useful and helpful. One is encouraged to turn to God in times of need or joy, to pour out one's heart, to take hold of that helping hand, to pray for healing. I call this the "It couldn't hurt" approach. While it is benevolent, it still begs the question.

There are also many people—good people, and I meet them every day—who declare themselves to be "not religious" but who perform acts of love and kindness and righteousness toward others. There are others who appear to be religious, who study Torah, but who do all manner of unethical things, are nasty to others, and lead lives that are unworthy of emulation. The implication is clear. What good is religion and belief in God if it produces people like that? Such people make it difficult for me to insist on the necessity of God. Besides, I do not want to disabuse the ethical humanist of his faith in people. Actions do speak louder than words. For me, one who does God's work in the world by loving and caring for others, even if he or she does not place God in the mix, is worthy of praise. But I just do not think it is enough.

All of us people of faith have to be open to the possibility that we created God. I own that. But there is another possibility, equally compelling—that we are God's creation and that the story we have been telling for as long as there have been people is essentially true. We may tell that story in many ways. We may describe God as a process, a force, a power, or an intelligence. Or we may use anthropomorphic imagery, which helps us humanize and feel closer to this transcendent God. In whatever way we say it, we admit that we and everything else are the result of God's creative energy in the universe. There is a power greater than ourselves, infinite and endless, that always was, is, and will be. God is the primary reality, that which connects you and me, and all creation for all time. What we call ONE.

And if this is what we believe—and here it gets a bit threatening for us—it means we have to accept our limits. It means we are not in control, at least not ultimate control. It means the world does not revolve around us and our needs any more than the sun revolves around the earth. For us in the modern world, this may feel like (you should pardon the expression) heresy. After all, hasn't the experience of modernity been about our controlling our own fate, our own destiny? We have displaced God from the center of the universe and then from the center of our lives. And in God's place? None other than you and I, our thoughts and beliefs, our ideals and creations, our wants and needs. To accept God means we must return to a theocentric view of the universe and life itself. This means God is firmly in the center. Not you or I. And that scares us, for it makes us recognize that we are not in control.

But that is the other possibility. There is no absolute certainty. The best we can do is stake a claim and live accordingly, live as if there is (or there isn't) God. Make your choice and place your bets. Personally, I stake my claim on the former. It just seems to make more sense to me—always has. From the time I was a little boy, standing next to my grandpa in synagogue, playing with the fringes on his tallis, wrapping it around my shoulders, I felt held by God. I was the religious child in a household that lived and breathed Jewish culture but was very secular. We talked about the Jewish people, ate Jewish foods, sent care packages to Israel, but there was no talk about God or religion in my home. Not unlike many New York Jews of the time. Even then, without the words to express it, I knew I would rather wager my life that there is God and then try to live accordingly.

Why? And why should you invest all that time, energy, and focus if it turns out that there really isn't God in the first place? Well, I wish I could say your life would always be happier, that you would never get angry or hurt the ones you love, that you would always have clarity of purpose and direction, that having God in your life would be a recipe for happiness, security, and inner peace. For many prophets, the presence of God was like a "fire in the bones," driving them more than a bit crazy, isolating them from their fellow human beings.

The truth is, our having faith in God's reality does not free us from our humanity and the foibles associated with being a person. We will still be imperfect. Faith will not make us instantly good; it may just make us a little "less bad." But faith does give us a way to pick ourselves up again, to know the difference between good and evil and thus to feel responsible for, but not condemned by, our mistakes. It locates us in a community of others, fellow travelers to support and sustain us. It attaches us to timeless values that are not subject to every trend and whim that comes along. It provides us a code of conduct, a framework within which we can measure and structure our lives. It guides us in the choices we make, from how and what we eat to how we spend our time and money. It provides us with a sense of purpose and mission. It helps us to feel that we are never alone. In the end, I believe, faith in God makes more sense, it makes the world a better place, it makes my life work better.

Not to believe in God, for me, is a much shakier proposition. Then what? Where will ultimate authority reside? In you and me? I know myself too well. I know that I am capable of much good, truly altruistic behavior, but I also know I am capable of rationalizing away all my faults and my failures. We all are. Besides, each of us is so wrapped up in our own life, our own feelings of want and entitlement, that our view can only be subjective, is bound to be motivated by self-interest and survival. And when it comes to those we love, or causes that we support, we have to admit, objectivity is out the window.

I am even less convinced that "society" can be the authority. In our own time, have we not witnessed majority-mandated evil? We have seen governments in so-called enlightened and educated nations legislate torture, genocide, and terrorism. The greatest atrocities against humanity have been committed in this century by governments that have outlawed religion and exiled God. And if there is no God, who will say that murder is wrong, or that anything is wrong? And how will we know that the highest value is to love my neighbor as I would myself want to be loved? Or is that just someone else's opinion? All anthropocentric systems are bound to fail, given the reality of self-interest. Because, in the right set of circumstances, self-interest will tell us that we are exempt from following the rules of conscience. And if we do not have an Ultimate Authority that resides above all persons and any human institution, an authority that tells us what we must do, then we will violate any rule. Just one night of watching the local news will tell you that.

But it goes beyond that. If there is no God, to whom will we pray? Where will we turn when friends and family are not available? Who will heal us when we are wounded and broken? Who will give us courage and strength when our own personal resources fail us? In what can we hope? Where is the authority for all our worthy behavior? Is it just that it feels right? What happens if it no longer does? How do we respond to those who declare that it is a cold, cruel, dog-eat-dog world, and we must look out for number one? Is it just that we disagree? One opinion versus another, with each person entitled to his or her own opinion? Is life really any deeper, richer, more meaningful without God? I don't think it can be.

A story is told of a wedding taking place in a storefront restaurant. The musicians are off in an alcove and so cannot be seen from the street. Two deaf men walk by and see all these people jumping and dancing with wild abandon. One turns to the other and signs that these people in the restaurant must be crazy; the deaf men, of course, could not hear the music.

Yes, there may be no God. Or there just might be, even if we cannot personally "hear the music." That's just the way it is for some of us. Whatever you believe does not make you a bad person. Nevertheless, I choose to live my life as if there is God. For right now, in spite of all the abuses perpetrated in God's name, I don't think we can do any better. Those who want to know for sure before they stake their own claim, will have to wait for a long time. If we could know with absolute certainty, we would not have to call it faith.

Question 2

What Is the Nature of God?

"I thought God was all-loving. But then how could an all-loving God allow such a tragedy to occur?" came the challenge in a session I was leading. "What makes you think God is all-loving?" I responded. Confused, he replied, "Well, I thought He was."

The problem here, and it exists in lots of our God talk, is that we come to God with preconceived notions of what the Holy One is and is not. We have inherited, each of us, from our religious school training, from our reading of the prayer book, a variety of notions concerning the nature of God. We "see" God through the particular prism of our being, telling more about ourselves than about God. Each of us is a receptacle, a filter. So as adults, when the God we encounter in a Torah text or the one we meet in the world does not live up to the rather narrow box that we have created, or that was created for us, then we want to reject God as somehow false. The real challenge, though, is for us to examine our definitions, and attempt to come to the God relationship without our preconceptions.

So many of us suffer from what I call the Dispenser Machine

God. We think that all we have to do is go to the machine, put in our coins (prayers), and out will come whatever it is we asked for. When we don't get it, we begin to feel there really was no dispenser machine after all. But just like a good parent, sometimes the most loving answer God can give us is "no."

The problem of creating God in our own image is not a new one. After their initial encounter, Moses returns to God and asks for God's name. "Tell me who You are so that I can go back and tell the others." Moses wants God's business card, concrete proof that he has had a God experience, one that he can talk about to others. He needs to demonstrate the reality both to himself and to those who will ask about it. He feels that if He has a name, then the experience was real.

God responds to Moses, "*Eh-hee-yeh ah-sher eh-hee-yeh*. Tell them *Eh-hee-yeh* is the One who sent you." Though you may see that translated any number of ways, the literal translation (which in this case is the most appropriate) is "I will be that which I will be. Tell them I will be sent you." This is not the answer Moses wants. God does not always give us what we want. But it is the most honest answer. God's self-naming, self-definition is *Be-ing coming into Be-ing.* God is a not-yet moment, not finite, not a noun, not some thing that we can limit in some way. God is not a what or a who; God is a when. Or an almost when. A moment that is always almost about to happen. That is the true nature of God, a higher understanding. But not that easy to talk about. In God's self-revelation, we hear that God cannot be limited to a name. We use names. In fact, our tradition says there are seventy names by which we can call upon God. But we always need to understand that, just as with us, none of these names equals God.

William Shakespeare's famous disclaimer aside—"What's in a name? That which we call a rose by any other word would smell as sweet" (*Romeo and Juliet*)—a name is a limitation, a definition, an attempt on our part to say who someone is and is not. When I say I am Terry Allen Bookman, son of Arthur and Lillian, I am no longer any man. I am identified as a specific person. But at the same time I am not contained in that name; it does not—it cannot—tell you everything about me. Besides, I have many names, even different names for different occasions. Some know me as Rabbi, others as *abba* (Hebrew for Daddy), still others as Tuvyah. I am all of these and none of them. And what is true for me is also true for you, for all of us. Our names are important, but they only tell a small piece of our stories.

The biblical tradition forbids the making of graven images— no pictures or statues may be made of God. Why? Because we cannot literally make such a statue. The statue cannot be "of God" it can be only of our concept of God. Oh, just like the prophets, poets, and artists of every age, we can use our artistic talents, and even our literary talents. We can make things that move the heart and the spirit. If we want to communicate about God, what choice do we have? Nevertheless, nothing we write, nothing we draw, nothing we sculpt can ever be God.

The problem with such images, and the problem with symbols and names in general, is that we begin to substitute or mistake them for the real thing. God becomes love, or a kindly old man sitting on a throne. We become so attached to our images that we forget they are supposed to be utilized only for their evocative power. God resists this temptation by telling Moses the only true name. The Israelites could not hear it because their spirits had been crushed (Exodus 6:9); they wanted an image. Later, because they had not yet evolved to this higher understanding that God is without definition, they would make one.

We are, each of us, evolving toward that higher understanding. In our path are many stumbling blocks. Our desire for concrete knowledge, available to us in some disciplines, is simply unavailable to us in our quest for God. There is something inherently unknowable about God; something inherently other. I don't even know myself all the time. When it comes to another human being, the same frustration also exists. After nineteen years of marriage, Karen and I still are discovering new things about each other, and as I age, I come more and more to accept the reality that I just won't ever know everything. Our relationship with God is infinitely more mysterious.

This would be good advice to follow in all our relationships. The people we meet are rarely who or what we think them to be. What they are is both more fascinating and more disappointing than we could ever imagine. When I facilitate a pre-marriage counseling session, I tell couples that while change is inevitable, they should enter marriage assuming that the person they are marrying will be the same person for the rest of their lives. It is amazing to me how many people still hold on to the notion that they will change their partner for the "better" (i.e., what they want that person to be) after the wedding.

The qualities that our tradition does identify with God are spelled out in God's self-revelation to Moses, later in the Book of Exodus. This same descriptor is then ensconced in the liturgy of all the Jewish festivals. When we take out the Torah on these holy days, we chant, quoting Exodus, "Adonai, Adonai, a God of compassion and grace, slow to anger, filled with loving-kindness and truth, showing mercy for a thousand generations, forgiving iniquity, transgression, and sin, but in no way clearing the guilty in that the sins of one generation will be found in their children and their children's children and grandchildren" (Exodus 34:6–7). This may not be the God we want, or even imagined. But it is God's self-revelation to us.

God is more complex than we might have imagined. Adonai is a God of loving-kindness but also a God of truth. This God can get angry, punish us, even our children and grandchildren, for our sins. God forgives us, but there are limits. I remember when my dad used to get riled up if we kids were being obnoxious. There was always a point when one of us went past the limit and he went after us. That is what I think of when I read this description. And then, after we were punished or spanked, and he'd had an opportunity to calm down, he would come to our room to hug and kiss us. "Why are you kissing them if you just hit them?" my incredulous mother would almost always say. "I hit them for what they did; I hugged them because I love them." My dad, like God, was capable of many emotions, even the extremes. And when I look out into the world, with its beauty and its ugliness, it seems to me that the God who is the Lord of the Universe is multidimensional, never easy to pin down to a single quality. Does this fit your own experience of the world?

What do we do when people tell us who they are and it does not fit our image or expectation? What do we say? Do we deny their reality of themselves, preferring to stick to our own? Or do we try to make room in our minds and hearts for what they say about themselves? And when our experience of them causes us to question their words or our preconceived images, are we capable of expanding the box into which we have placed and labeled them? In an ever-changing, dynamic universe, God, too, evolves and changes. That may not be what we wanted, but it is what we got. God is what *God* will be. Now and forever.

Question 3

~

Why Do Bad Things Happen to Good People?

And Why Do Bad Things Happen in Our World?

One of the most difficult questions any religious system must answer centers around the existence of evil and its consequences in our world. In theology departments, we call it "theodicy," and entire courses are devoted to it. As one who ministers to and counsels people when they are in pain over a loss or a tragedy, I have come to understand that while explanations may sound good on paper, they are all incomplete or limited. This is especially true in the face of another's pain. At those moments I try to avoid all explanations. It is time for our hearts, our tears, and our hugs, not for intellectual understanding and smart answers. There will be time to reflect. When tragedy or illness or death strikes, I attempt to be present as pastor, as rabbi, as friend, not as scholar or writer.

One of the things about Judaism that sometimes drives us and others crazy is that we have almost no dogmas when it comes to issues of belief. We are doctrinally open, which means that we are free to believe just about anything within the boundary of monotheism. So there is no one authoritative Jewish answer to these questions. But I can lay out a bunch of different perspectives for you. As you read them, it might feel like your first philosophy or psychology class. I remember declaring I was a Platonist the first week—until we read Aristotle. Others followed. I wound up an existentialist because that was what we studied last. Feel free to pick and choose the answers that work best for you as you read through these. You may wind up with a hybrid response— mostly I believe this, but I also think that. You may even want to think about it some more. If this is one of the most difficult questions about God, then you are entitled to take your time in answering it. One thing, though: Your answer to this question will be influenced by and needs to be in sync with any previous decisions you have made about the nature and reality of God. For example, if you believe that God is all-powerful, then you need to ask, "Why didn't God stop the evil?" On the other hand, if God is not all-powerful, "What is the source of the evil?" There are always questions.

The Sins of Society

We as a community have sinned, have strayed from the path that God has set for us, and so we are being punished collectively. This is the classic Jewish response, etched in the words of the prophets: "Because of our sins, we have been exiled from our land." When something bad happens, when disaster strikes, the traditional Jewish response is to look within and ask, What have "we" done? Our guilt and responsibility are collective. And God chooses the instrument of our punishment, whether it be an invading army or a so-called natural disaster.

When this response is applied to our own time, it can be said that we are stricken with cancer because human beings have degraded the environment to such a degree, through pollution and overdevelopment, that people are getting sick. Taken a step further, one may understand such diseases of modern life as God's response, through nature, to the sins of society.

Do "innocent" individuals also suffer because society fails to act morally? All the time. Gun violence, drunk driving, lack of care for the mentally ill—these and other acts bring tragedy to our world every day. And on some level we do bear responsibility for such sins of society. In a post-Holocaust age, it is inexcusable to say, "I knew nothing" or "I was only obeying orders." We have to own our communal responsibility.

In the Torah we find this amazing passage that asks the question "What do you do if you find a murdered body in a field, away from any town or settlement?" Well, after taking care of the corpse, the elders of the nearby towns measure the distance to the closest village. Everyone there must contribute to the burial of the body. After that, they must bring a communal guilt and sin offering for allowing such an act to take place and not doing enough to prevent it. Compare that to the nightly parade of victims in our own city streets, about which we merely shrug our shoulders and add up the body count. The notion that we all bear responsibility and may be punished for the sins of others is found throughout Jewish tradition, especially in the liturgy of the High Holy Days.

The Sins of the Parents

In the Ten Commandments we read that the sins of the parents (literally, the "father") are visited upon the children up to the third or fourth generation. Most of us, when we read it, are struck by how unfair this sounds, and even though the same verse reports that obedience is rewarded for a thousand generations, we are not appeased. Yet how true this sometimes is.

When I am counseling someone about such issues as alcoholism, chemical addiction, child or spouse abuse, philandering, or deep hostility among family members, I invariably ask, "Did you ever see anything like this as a child?" I am no longer surprised by the number of those who answer "Yes," who have "inherited" family "sins" and are stuck unconsciously honoring their parents by repeating patterns they learned as children. In addition, we all know of children born with a variety of problems because of something the mother did during pregnancy. And while genetic inheritance of problems is not to be understood as sin, it does help us explain some instances of human suffering. Though this biblical passage may not answer every single instance of a bad thing happening to a good person, it does seem to offer a partial explanation.

The Individual Is Being Punished

While collective guilt might explain some situations, the Book of Job raises the stakes on this question by asking, "What about when there is no collective guilt and it is not the community that is being punished, but an individual, a good person, who is suffering? Can we say that suffering is always the result of sin and punishment?" For that is what happens to the biblical character Job. He is a good man who "fears God and shuns evil." But the "Adversary" challenges God by saying that Job is a believer only because God has blessed him in every way. "Take away that which is his, and he will certainly blaspheme You to Your face," so Job has everything systematically taken away from him—work, home, possessions, health, even his family. Clearly he was not being punished; yet, he was certainly suffering.

Nevertheless, and in spite of Job's dismissal, one possible response is that good and evil are rewarded and punished respectively by a God who is concerned with justice. While it might appear that the person who suffers is good, she or he has, in fact, committed some sins for which God is now meting out punishment.

Personally, while I like the notion that goodness is rewarded and evil is punished, I have to admit that I have some problems with this one. Once I heard it pronounced by a rabbi at the tragic death of a young woman killed by a drunk driver. "Who knows," the rabbi intoned, "what sins she may have committed?" Though I am certain he was coming from his own theology on the subject, I felt like strangling him, right there at the cemetery. At least if I had, we would have known for what sins he had died—the sins of incredible insensitivity and causing pain to those already suffering and in need of comfort.

The Individual Is at Fault

While the person may not literally have "sinned," there may have been something in his/her lifestyle or behavior that caused the tragedy. For example, if a person has a heart attack, one might be able to explain it by pointing to the fact that s/he was overweight, did not exercise, worked too much in stress-filled situations, and the like. While I am appalled at those who imply that sexually transmitted diseases are God's punishments for sex outside the strict confines of marriage, I do believe that anyone who practices unsafe sex these days is courting disaster. On this and other issues, we can often say that if the person had done the "right things," then the problem might have been averted. The individual has to own some degree of personal responsibility.

Only God Knows

When tragedy or something terrible occurs, we often find it beyond human comprehension that it even happened. Usually we find it impossible to come up with any plausible explanation. Nevertheless, some people's faith requires an answer—that God must have had a reason even though they cannot understand it. Sometimes, this response is extended further to the notion that we human beings have no right to question God's motives. God acts in mysterious ways. God has a will, a plan for each of us. This is the final "answer" given in the Book of Job. God silences Job by rhetorically asking, "Were you there when I created the heavens and the earth?" The implication is that only the Creator has the right and the knowledge of when things and people ought to come to be and when their time on earth is up. As wonderful as we human beings are, our vision and understanding are limited. From the human or personal perspective, what looks like evil to us may merely be the natural consequences of life itself. Thus, an earthquake may be a disaster for those who chose to live on the fault line, but it is merely the earth's way of maintaining itself through shifting plates deep beneath the surface. A river flooding, a forest fire, a volcano—all these events are necessary for the planet to survive. Even bacteria and other biological "evils" are necessary for our body's health. When kept in check, they perform functions that help keep us alive.

Yet Judaism has a strong tradition of calling God to task, of challenging God's decisions. When you have an intimate, trusting relationship with another, you can tell him/her that you don't agree with, or like, or approve of what he or she is doing without threatening the relationship itself. The Jewish people have always conceived of their relationship with God as eternal. Though the bonds are often stretched, they cannot be broken. So it is not uncommon for us to challenge or question God when we are knocked down.

I was teaching a class in Wisdom literature as part of a continuing education program for Catholic educators. I had shared Job's challenging of God, his calling God to task for his own inexplicable suffering after living what he considered to be a life of good deeds. One of my students, an elderly nun, had a difficult time with Job's not accepting God's will. We talked about it a great deal, even after class, and I could see that she was struggling with the very notion that a human being could even question God's decisions for us. A few months later I received a note from her. She was driving along a deserted road late one night when she decided to take up Job's method of challenging God. It seems there was a certain family in her parish, good people, who were experiencing one problem after another. She was chastising God on their behalf when suddenly her tire blew out. She made it safely to the side of the road, bemoaning her abandonment of what she knew to be the correct path of acceptance. Then, from out of nowhere, a young man pulled up behind her, changed the tire, and left, without her so much as getting his name. She wrote: "So in the end, I am not sure which was God's answer to me—the tire or the young man." And then she added a postscript: "Nevertheless, I will not be taking up that line of argument with God again."

A Test

In the life of every great spiritual leader, from Moses to Jesus to the Buddha, there was always a time in which he was tested. These tests often took place in a desert, on a mountain, or in the wilderness—each situation involving an extended time during which that leader felt all alone, abandoned, challenged in his beliefs and faith. Sometimes people believe that bad things are tests of our faith or our character. When we suffer—and we all do at one point or another in our lives—we are challenged to face the pain with courage and dignity. We can view such moments as God testing us or simply "tests of life." By enduring the suffering and coming through on the other side, we can build character and deepen our bonds of faith. In a sense, we are gross metal, being refined by the fires of life's negative challenges. Somehow it is through this refining process that we learn life's most important lessons, those that are necessary for our spiritual growth.

I remember a climbing expedition that went wrong. Because of some very heavy weather I was separated from my climbing partner, and I decided to return to base camp. Never good with directions, and without a compass, I became disoriented and lost in the fog. I soon found myself descending through the brush and wound up in waist-deep swampy water. Cold, wet, without food, and lost in a wilderness area, I was fully aware that I could die. While accepting that possibility, I asked God for the strength to keep my legs moving. After more than twelve hours of walking, I found a trail and made it out of the forest. I know I was tested that day. The lessons I learned about myself, about life, about God, have stayed with me ever since. That day, I "knew" that God was with me, that God wanted my life to continue. When I was totally exhausted and ready to give up, it was God's power that kept me moving, kept me alive. There's no other way to explain it. I learned that I was not alone in this world, that none of us are. I faced my fear and lived to tell about it. It would not be the last time, and as I reflected back, I realized it was not the first time either. God had been a presence in my life, is a presence in all our lives. We can be oblivious to that reality. We can even deny it. Nevertheless, God waits for us and for our acknowledgment. The Holy One is very patient.

Good Will Ultimately Result

There was a rabbi in the Talmud who, no matter what befell him, would say, *"Gahm zoo l'toe-vah/*This will also be for the good!"* As a result, he was known as Rabbi Gahm Zoo. Many of us have faith that in the end, things will turn out all right; everything will be for the better. We look for the good that is hidden in the bad that occurs, and we look forward to better times. Many times I have seen a family or a couple brought together by a crisis. One of the most successful businessmen I ever met had been fired from his middle-management position in a major corporation. Suddenly, everything for which he had been working was shattered. But because of it, he formed his own company, created new products and concepts, and wound up a wealthy and very happy man. The day he was fired was the lowest point in his life. Yet none of his success would have happened had he not been fired.

In yoga it is taught this way: without pain there is no gain. (It also says, "Do not go seeking pain; it will find you.") Life batters and bruises us as we live it. But just as in the natural world, such apparent disasters become the very ground for future life and abundance.

Sometimes Evil Wins/God Is Not All-Powerful

Though we have been taught that God is omnipotent, perhaps that is not the case. Perhaps God cannot, does not, control all the happenings of the universe. We might say that God is not a micro-manager. God simply does not have that kind of control, deciding each day who will get cancer, who will be in an accident, who will hit a home run in the baseball game.

In addition, there is evil, a real and powerful force that does have limited and temporary dominance in the world as we know it. Ultimately, good will win. But for that, we will have to wait for the messianic time.

For There to Be Happiness, There Must Be Sadness

My sister, Frada, used to say to me whenever I was sad, or disappointed, or hurt by another's actions, that when you are sensitive, the highs are higher and the lows are lower. You cannot get one without the other; otherwise, all life is flat, without feeling, without emotion. So I asked her, "Is it worth it, all this pain?" She responded, "Absolutely!"

There is a balance of good and bad things happening in this world, and we would be incapable of knowing the one without experiencing the other. We must suffer so that we can, at other times, rejoice. To everything, to every experience, there is a moment in time. God gives and God takes away. That is the reality of each of our lives, all our lives.

Fate or Luck

Judaism is big on free will. Over and over again we are taught that while God wants us to choose goodness and life, we do have choices. Yet, at times, there seems to be a bit of destiny at work as well. In Yiddish we have the word *ba-sheert,* which means "it was meant to be." It is usually used for happy things, such as when a couple meets under unlikely circumstances and winds up getting married. But it can also be used to describe something terrible. I remember reading a story about a guy on his way home from work who pulled into a parking lot to call home. He finished his call by telling his wife that he would see her soon, and then an airplane fell from the sky and landed on his car, killing him instantly. Was it meant to be?

We could also say it was just plain bad luck. *Mazel* is a term used quite often in Jewish circles, as in *Mazel tov!* (literally, "Good luck!" but also used for "Congratulations!") Actually, the word *mazel* refers to the constellations. Originally, then, it might have meant something like, "May your signs and constellations all be aligned in the proper place." Interesting for a religious tradition that is supposed to be so rational and intellectual. No matter what we say, however, some people do seem to have bad luck. Things just never go their way. And things happen to all of us from time to time. Like the bumper sticker says, LIFE HAPPENS. There is a certain amount of randomness in the world, as if it was in the mix of creation. Not everything can follow according to the rules or the plan. In my experience in visiting the sick, I can tell you that while there may be a genetic propensity toward certain diseases, and lifestyle will influence our health, I have seen too many people struck down by illness (especially cancer) for which there was no other explanation than "bad luck."

Life Is Not Always Fair

We have an expectation of fairness. It seems right that each of us ought to be treated fairly by God, by life, by others. But our experience teaches us that such is not always the case. Some people just seem to carry more burdens or suffer more than others. While there may be balance to all this pain on the societal or communal level, it does not necessarily trickle down to the individual. Does God give us only what we can handle? Who knows? Nevertheless, I have found that the old Yiddish expression "If we each hung our troubles out on a clothesline, we would all wind up taking our own back into the house" rings true.

At the same time, we are challenged to protest God's injustice, just as Abraham did when told of the plan to destroy Sodom and Gomorrah: "Would You destroy an entire city if there could be found fifty righteous men therein?"

Olam haBah/*World to Come*

I think the question I have most often been asked by other Jews is, "We don't believe in an afterlife, do we?" The answer is that though conceptualizations have changed throughout the centuries, Judaism has always held that bodily death is not the end. There is an eternality built into every human being that continues after our physical demise. In the Bible it was called Sheol, a kind of underworld where all spirits continue to dwell for eternity. By the time of the rabbis, when Jews were living under brutal Roman persecution, a fully developed system of heaven (called *olam haBah* or *Gan Eden*) and hell (called *gehenna*) was promulgated. This world stinks. In this world, by its very nature, the righteous suffer, and the evil who care only for themselves get all the breaks. But in the next world the tables will be turned and the righteous of all faiths will be rewarded for their good deeds, while the evil will be punished. This condition will continue to the end of days, when all, good and evil alike, will come to know and acknowledge the One God.

This response to suffering in this world was later downplayed by the rabbis, as it became a cornerstone of faith in the emerging Catholic Church.

God Suffers with Us

A number of years ago a reading was going around that consisted of a man speaking to God about his life: "God, throughout my life, when things were going well, I walked with You and You walked with me, for whenever I looked down, there were two sets of footprints in the sand. Yet last year, when things went poorly, whenever I looked down there was only one set of footprints. Why did You abandon me in my time of need?" And God responded, "My son, when you looked down and saw but one set of footprints . . . those were mine, for I was carrying you."

When bad things happen to us, God watches and is saddened by our pain. As part of our covenantal relationship, God suffers with us and seeks to comfort us. While God cannot stop bad things from happening, the Compassionate One walks alongside us, carries us through all our joys and sorrows.

～

After the Temple was destroyed in Jerusalem, Adonai sent the *Sheh-chee-nah*, the feminine indwelling presence of God, to accompany us in all our trials and tribulations. That presence is still available to us if only we avail ourselves of it. When pain and loss assail us, we do well to ask God to help us get through it. To this prayer there is always an affirmative response.

Y'soo-reen Shell Ah-hah-vah/*The Sufferings of Love*

We have all heard the line "This is going to hurt me more than it will hurt you" and none of us has ever believed it until we became parents and we learned that there are times when our children must be punished or disciplined for their own good. We do it, not out of anger or meanness, but because it is necessary at that moment.

〜

There is a Jewish notion, developed during periods of deep suffering on the part of our people, that our pain was inflicted by God as a necessary element of God's love for us. According to this notion, God is compelled to cause us to suffer (usually through the hand of an enemy or natural disaster) so that we will stop our sinful ways and return to our relationship with the Holy One. Another way of understanding this is to say that we sometimes suffer because, as loyal servants of the One God, we are persecuted and attacked by others. At times, it is our love of God that brings us hardship and pain.

God Is Indifferent to, or Ignores Human Suffering

Is it possible that God merely created us, gave us a rule book (the Torah) and then left us alone to take care of ourselves? God the disinterested Creator? Or, is God so busy taking care of the universe that sometimes we are temporarily ignored or forgotten?

In the Book of Exodus, chapter 6, God says, "Now I have heard the groaning of my people and remembered My covenant." Now? What had God been doing for the previous four hundred years? And in God's absence, or lack of focused concern, we suffered mightily.

In the holiday of Purim, one of the customs is to mask ourselves. In the entire story of Esther, God's name does not appear even once. Playing on the name Esther in Hebrew, the rabbis said that Purim was a time of "*hess-teer panim*/hiding of the face." Whose face? God's. Which is why we hide our own faces during the holiday. Sometimes God hides from us. It is then our challenge to act like Mordechai and Esther and take matters into our own hands. It has been argued that we live in a time of *hess-teer panim;* that God is hidden from us and that we must make extraordinary efforts to seek out God's presence in our lives.

Work Is Done

Each of us has a task, a purpose, a reason for being born into the world. And when that work is completed, our lives are ended. It is difficult to know just what that work is, and we never know how long we have to complete it. For some, it might be just a single day. For others, ninety or more years. Longevity is not promised to any one of us.

Several years ago I worked with a teenager who was dying of leukemia. He had made a list of all the things he wanted to accomplish with his life, and when he checked everything off, he told me he was ready to leave his body. On the last day of his brief life, he was in a coma. Suddenly his eyes opened and he sat bolt upright in bed, stretching his arms toward the ceiling of his bedroom. He said, "Take me home," and then he lay back down and died. I will never forget what he taught me.

～

All of these approaches have problems and are limited. If any one of them resonates with you, someone will invariably say, "What about . . . ?" and we will not have an answer. None of them works in a moment of true suffering. The next time some tragedy occurs to someone you know, don't say, "It is because . . ." At the moment of our friends' pain, our task is to comfort them, hold their hands, hug them, cry with them, provide for their needs, be with them. Nothing more. Nothing less. Don't provide explanations or theology lessons. Don't even give them this chapter to read. Just be a loving friend.

Why Are There No Miracles Today?
Why Doesn't God Still Speak to Us?

Ten-year-old Jessica came to my study to ask me some questions she had been wondering about for quite some time. After I checked in with her about school, her family, and her varied sports activities, I said to her, "So, I hear you have some questions for me?" Without hesitation she asked, "If God took the Jewish people out of Egypt, why didn't He create a miracle and rescue us from the Holocaust? The Torah says God spoke to Moses. Why doesn't God speak to us anymore?"

I thanked her for asking me these questions. It is truly a blessing to know that children feel so comfortable with themselves and their religious struggles that they are willing to open up in this way. After stating that her questions were really addressing God and could be asked directly (with which she agreed), I took a stab at answering. It was not the first time I had been asked such questions. The same questions, in various forms, are asked in my adult classes, but never with such earnestness as this ten-year-old girl displayed. As a rabbi, I am seen as God's representative here on earth. I work for the company. I need to answer for its failures, both real and imagined.

I asked Jessie how she knew there were no miracles, how she knew that God does not speak to us. Are miracles only when seas part, or are there in fact little miracles, surrounding us each day, that go unnoticed? Babies are born, my body performs millions of functions without any input from me, flowers bloom, patients are inexplicably cured of dreadful diseases, while flying in an airplane I communicate with someone thousands of miles away using a little box called a computer—are these not miracles? In our daily prayer book there is a listing of blessings to be recited upon awakening, titled *"Nee-seem b'chol yohm/*Daily Miracles." These blessings thank God for the ability to perform such acts as opening our eyes after a night's sleep, taking our first steps, putting on a bathrobe, stretching, and so on. They are there to remind us not to take anything for granted, not to assume that what we do each day is automatic, part of nature. Just ask someone who has been hospitalized for a period of time. When he or she is able to get up from that bed, walk to the bathroom, eat solid food, those so-called ordinary acts feel like the miracles they truly are.

Miracles have a great deal to do with perception. This is taught in the biblical story of Moses and the burning bush. Moses, the shepherd, is out grazing his sheep. As he searches for a straying lamb, he sees a bush burning off in the distance. Now, a bush burning in a high desert like Sinai is a rather common occurrence. The extreme heat and the dry climate combine to create the conditions under which spontaneous combustion of dried plants can take place. What is unusual is that Moses stops to watch it. And only when he stops does he realize that the bush is not being consumed (i.e., that a miracle is taking place). There are bushes burning around us all the time. The question is, do we ever stop to look at them? If we did, the Torah seems to indicate, God would be waiting for us.

But some of us are not satisfied with that. We want big

miracles that no one can deny. Where are our seas that part? Where is the hand of God intervening in the natural course of things, defying nature, making believers of us all? Perhaps those kinds of miracles are not meant to happen more than once in a people's history. After all, nearly four thousand years later we are still repeating that story each and every year at Passover. It helped to shape us as a people, defining who and what we are.

That being said, I am not so sure that big miracles have ceased altogether. What do we call it when a plane crashes, is sheared in two, and everyone walks away with only minor injuries? Or an earthquake hits at night, destroying a bridge that during the day would have been carrying thousands of commuters? Some, I am sure would call such things luck, or fate, or accidents of nature. And perhaps they are. I choose to call them miracles. Who knows?

Besides, contrary to popular belief, miracles do not create believers out of us. Only three months after crossing the Sea of Reeds and forty days after hearing the voice of God at Mount Sinai, the people created a calf of gold and called it "God", bowed down to it, worshipped it. Miracles do not equal faith. Our Torah reminds us of that fact. And anyone who has witnessed a miracle can just as easily talk himself out of it. *Did I really see it? I don't know. It was kind of dark out, and there was so much pushing and shoving going on. I had eaten that weird meal and maybe it was indigestion, or perhaps I dreamed it. It was so long ago. I just can't be sure. No one else saw it, so I really don't know.* We fool ourselves by thinking that if only we could witness a miracle then we would be certain of God's continued existence. It just isn't so.

I love the chutzpah of the person who asks, "If God spoke to Moses, then why doesn't God speak to me?" Do you realize what it takes to ask such a question? The sense that one is on par with one of the greatest spiritual figures of all time. The possibility exists that a Moses is a once-in-a-people's-history occurrence. No one has ever attained the same status since, and probably no one ever will. But I do believe that God is speaking to us all the time. It is kind of like a radio. The station broadcasts morning till night, but if we do not have our radios on, or if we are tuned in to the wrong station, we hear nothing. And when we do turn them on, if we do not tune them in precisely, if we are even one tiny band off, all we hear is muffled sound and static.

The Jewish tradition poses that God speaks to us with two voices. The loud voice, the unmistakable voice, the one that gets all the press, is the one that spoke to us at Mount Sinai. There, all the people stood, while the mountain shook, flames shot up, and God spoke. According to the rabbis, every soul that ever was or ever will be was present at Sinai. Thus, in each of us resides a memory of that moment in time. On the holy day of Shavuot, we reenact that moment by standing to hear the Ten Commandments read aloud.

But lest we forget and romanticize that moment, remember that loud voice so terrified us that we begged for it to stop. *Moses, you go and listen to that voice and tell us what to do. We will do it and then understand it. Just tell it to stop!* The loud voice is scary; it overwhelms us. Perhaps that is why it occurs so rarely. Could we really hear it any better than they did at that mountain in the wilderness? I am not convinced we could.

There is another voice, however. The still, small voice within us, within us all. The prophet Elisha taught us about this voice long ago. It is the voice of conscience, the voice of knowing the right thing to do, the voice of intuition, the voice of God. What do we have to do to hear that voice? We have to listen inside. We have to shut up and quiet all the distractions, all the noise that has become so much a part of our lives that we do not even hear it anymore, all the interference, all the "head garbage," all the voices inside our heads and the ones outside as well. That is why every spiritual discipline in the history of the world includes silence and meditation. Those are practices that help us quiet the noise so that we can truly listen. Many of us feel that we have to get away from our daily routine in order to listen, and certainly the right setting can be a help. That is why we often feel closer to God in the outdoors or at a retreat. It is quieter. We can listen better. And if we listen, then we will hear.

When someone comes to me and says, "God is not speaking to me," my reply invariably is, "What kind of job are you doing of listening?" Usually the person is not doing very much—living a good, decent life and showing up at synagogue once in a while. I point out that unless God singles a person out in an act of grace, choosing him or her for some assignment or other, then it is very unlikely that he or she will ever hear the word of God. But if he or she works at it—and spirituality is work—then success will follow. In fact, I have rarely met a person, regardless of the spiritual discipline he or she has chosen, who consistently works on his or her relationship with God and still says, "I don't sense/feel/hear God in my life." I do hear that from lots of people who never walk into a house of worship, but not from those who do.

There are exceptions. I had been counseling a man who was a regular attendee at services. He was an attorney who did a great deal of pro bono work in the community, mild-mannered, nice family, whose wife and children were also involved in temple life. He just "didn't get this God thing." We talked on several occasions. In spiritual counseling, I always try to determine whether a person is having a content issue or a process issue. Part of the problem was language. He just did not relate to the liturgy of the prayer book. The notion of a God out there, high and mighty, judging all our actions, did not jive with his view of reality. Though I provided him another God image that helped (Mordechai Kaplan's force within us that leads us to good) and tried to move him from the verb "hear" to "sense," I don't think he ever felt any closer to God. And so it might be for some people. Even though they love the acts—coming to services, celebrating Shabbat and the holy days, doing acts of love and kindness on behalf of others—they just do not get the connection. Perhaps they never will. It could be a personality thing (he was into control) or it might be a proclivity that was absent in his case. Or it might just be that he was not ready, that his time will yet come. In the meantime, his actions are a force for good in his life and in the lives of others. I can live with that. I think he can, as well.

I utilize Torah stories because they provide us with all the psycho-spiritual questions we need for our own journeys through life. These stories become the mirror by which we can look at ourselves and do the work we need to do in our own lives. When Moses stopped to look at that burning bush, God was revealed to him for the first time. It was not something he was seeking. In fact, after all the turmoil of his life in the court of Pharaoh, Moses had settled into a quiet existence as a husband, father, and shepherd, son-in-law of the priest of Midian. It was a good life.

In Moses' encounter with God, there were many possible responses. He could have been skeptical—*Have I been out in the sun too long? Bushes don't speak; I am not hearing this. Was it the extra chili I put on my omelet this morning?* He could have simply asked, *Why me?* That is, in fact, what he does ask, trying to convince God that he has the wrong man for the job. He could have simply been frightened, afraid to even look at or listen to what was being revealed before his very eyes and ears. He could have been afraid of what such an encounter might mean in terms of his personal life—*Will I have to leave Midian? My pastoral existence? What about my wife and children?* He could have responded to God—*Why do You need me, a mere human being? If You are God, then You have the power. Why don't You take the people out of Egypt by Yourself?* Or, while he was not convinced of his own ability to carry out the chosen task, he could have been convinced that this was a God experience. And so he was.

If in your day, you have a God experience, think of how you might react. Think of how it might sound to your friends and family, or at the office. How do we know if it was a God experience or simply something we imagined, something inside of us? How do we explain anything that is incomparable, if not incomprehensible? Moses' life was radically changed by his encounter with God at the burning bush. It led to a lifetime of relationship between himself and the Holy One. So it is for all true God encounters. They cannot be denied. They change us forever. Our lives can never be the same. We cannot go back to living a "pre-God" life. Once you become convinced of the reality of God, you can try to deny it, pretend it did not happen, erase it from your memory, but you cannot go back. Moses could not go back to being a humble shepherd any more than we can live so-called "normal, secular lives" in which the main purpose is to fulfill ourselves and be happy. Perhaps that is why we seek to shut our eyes and stop up our ears. As if we could.

There are only two ways such an encounter can take place, and both require us to be open to God experiences. First, we seek God. Every religious tradition teaches methods for this to occur. In the second half of this book we will explore four Jewish paths. Second, God seeks us. We call this "grace." In other words, we can find God through our own spiritual praxis and development, or God can find us, tap us on the shoulder, call our name, create a miracle to draw our attention, or be revealed to us either suddenly or over time. A personal paradigm shift can be the result of our own work, or the result of the hand of God. Moses, a rather unlikely choice, an assimilated Jew who grew up in the royal palace, an escaped convict with a price on his head, a man with a speech impediment, a man married "out of the faith" to the daughter of a Midianite priest, was the one chosen by God to lead our people on the journey that would become the central story of our people and our faith. Go figure.

Even Moses was surprised by God's choice. There was nothing going on in his life that would have suggested it. No angst, no midlife crisis, no recent deaths in the family, no great losses. And so it is with us. We can never know when such a moment will occur. And if it does, if it already has, what was/will be your response? I am certain you are interested. Otherwise, you would not be reading this book.

Question 5

~

Seeing Is Believing, Right? Then Why Can't We See God?

Would seeing God really solidify your relationship with Him, to make it genuine, to have it become an everyday reality? What would it mean for you to be committed to that relationship, to accept its existence without question, to be sure of it and your role within it? Is it ever possible to be that confident of a spiritual relationship?

After escaping from Egypt, after crossing the Sea of Reeds and witnessing the revelation at Mount Sinai, and after the sin of the golden calf, the people of Israel are poised for Moses' return up the mountain. It is just then that Moses asks God for a concrete assurance of Adonai's ongoing presence in his life and the life of the people. Feeling a bit overwhelmed by the burden of leadership, Moses wants the assurance of God's help in leading the people forward. "Unless You go in the lead do not make us leave this place. For how shall it be known that Your people have gained Your favor unless You go with us?" (Exodus 33:15–16).

This is not about belief or doubt. Moses is beyond that. He knows God is real; he has heard the voice, seen the miracles, witnessed the Lord's saving power. What is it that he seeks, then? Moses wants an everyday relationship with God. He is no longer satisfied with momentary encounters, with burning bushes and smoking mountains, with God's dog-and-pony show. He wants God in an immanent relationship, not only with himself but with the people as well. It is as if Moses is saying to God, "You told me, You love me. Now show me. Be there for me." God acquiesces and says, "I will go in the lead."

Every leader or would-be leader has had this feeling on occasion. I know I have. I think about it every year when I go up to the ark to begin the High Holy Day services. There I stand, with all of my shortcomings, my failures. I am that chubby kid wearing huskies, that adolescent who was never going to feel like a man, that searcher who was going to wander forever. Now thousands of eyes are upon me, Rabbi Bookman, eyes looking to me for knowledge and confidence. Don't they see how really frightened I am? Don't they see I am still that little boy inside? "Oh, God. Help me get through this. Help me fill the shoes in which Your people have placed me. Help me be worthy of what You ask. Help me to help them in their time of need."

What makes the biblical story more interesting is that Moses does not stop there; he wants more. Like most of my counseling sessions, the real question is saved for last. This is not an ego trip for him—he's been there, he was in Pharaoh's court, he has been a success already. He is not looking for credit, personal gain, or any of the momentary satisfactions that might motivate one to seek power and leadership. And so he pushes it a step further. "Please, let me behold Your presence!" (Exodus 33:18). There comes a point in all intimate relationships where in order to continue the bond, it has to get deeper. It is as if there is no use in going on if the commitment is not total, not complete. Moses wants to raise the stakes, and if God is not willing to do so, he wants out. He asks to see God's "glory." He wants to see God.

What does it mean to "see" God? Doesn't Jewish tradition

maintain that God is without form, a non-object, a non-person, unlike anything we know? So how can such a God be seen? Certainly we are not talking about physical seeing, light flashing on the retina, an image being sent to the brain, and that image being interpreted. If we acknowledge that God is without physical form, then the kind of seeing we do with our eyes is not possible. Seeing, here, is a metaphor. Moses wants complete awareness and knowledge of God. Nothing less. He wants it all. And so do we.

What is it that you want from God? What will it take for you to have that absolute, solid certainty that God is a real event, the primary reality of the universe? Everyone has his or her own conditions. We all have our particular issues that prevent us from having God in our lives. *If only I could have a sign, a small miracle. If only God would speak to me. If, as I am driving to work one day, the light would shine in such a way that I would know it is truly the Lord, then I would believe.* We are all consciously or unconsciously laying out our conditions that, in the end, ironically enough, *prevent* us from relationship with God. And it isn't about belief or doubt, though those are the words we use. Rather, it is an issue of faith or trust. In this sense, this relationship parallels all our relationships. Without trust, trust in the other and trust in ourselves, trust in the relationship itself—that it can withstand whatever it is we will throw at it—no relationship can survive.

As much as God might love Moses—and when we love we want to do for the other—we cannot see God's "face" and be alive. We cannot "see" God in our present human state.* That level of knowledge of God is simply denied to us as human

---

*Though the text here is not explicit, it leaves open the possibility that we can see God in our "non-human," non-physical, or non-finite state. Such a possibility might help to explain the awareness of God in near-death experiences, dreams, out-of-body encounters, and in death itself. There are even some religious traditions that try to stimulate and guide these God encounters through the use of ritual and/or hallucinogenic substances.

beings. This is not the way we have been constructed or the universe created. We want it, but we cannot have it. We do have the ability to sense, to be aware of, to feel the presence, to learn about, to embrace, to believe and have faith in, but this level of absolute knowledge, of "face-to-face" encounter—this we are not going to get. Not because we aren't Moses. Not because we didn't get it right, study hard enough, meditate long enough, say the correct mantra, cross our legs and sit in the proper position, pray with the proper intention, do enough mitzvot on behalf of another. This is not about the proper effort. Rather, we cannot "see" God just because we are human beings.

As human beings, we are limited, finite, imperfect. Finite cannot assume the Infinite, cannot contain it. It is bigger than we are. At best we can get a glance, a peek, a piece of the totality—but not complete and absolute knowledge. Though Moses was no ordinary guy, he was still a human being. And as a human being, he had certain limitations. If you hold your hands in front of you, spread your fingers, and bring your hands together so that only two fingers overlap, you will have a visual image of our knowledge of God. There are points at which we touch. And there are gaps, as there are in all relationships, spaces in which we cannot know. Mystery. No human being, not even a Moses, has the capacity to bridge all the mysteries.

God does offer to Moses—and to us—"evidence of where I have been in this world," [the Hebrew word is *acharai,* usually mistranslated as "My back"] (Exodus 33:23), "but Me, Myself, you cannot see, you cannot have absolute knowledge. Your understanding of Me will always be partial. It will always be through where I have been."

You want to know God? Look *acharai,* look at what God's hands have touched. Look out into the world and see where God has been. Go ahead. Stop whatever you are doing and look around. Look at another person. Look out your window. Look in the mirror. Put your hand over your heart and feel its rhythmic beating.

See the little particles of dust dancing in the sunlight as it streams in through your window. Be aware of your mind reading these words, relating them to your own experience of the world. There are so many miracles to behold, so many pieces of evidence that God has been here. Each of us is a miracle, unique, no two exactly alike. Our very existence and individuality are evidence of *acharai,* of God's having been here in the world . . .

～

I used to *daven* (the Yiddish word for "pray") in the library of my former congregation. It was a beautiful room with two big picture windows looking out at a garden. In the garden were two wonderful trees and in the winter, while they lost their leaves, they retained berries, which fed the squirrels. I marveled at this tree that was alive and vibrant in every season of the year. One time, when chanting the *Aleinu* prayer, I bent my knees and bowed at the appropriate words. When I stood upright, I realized I was standing in front of the tree. Had I bowed down before a tree? Had I made an idol of it? The next time, I looked up at the sky. But was that any better? I shifted where I stood so I could be in front of the wall. Not only did that put me in front of the work of human hands, but it also took me away from looking out at the garden. Shutting my eyes made it no better. I was stuck with my internal images. Finally, it dawned on me that these are all reflections of the Creator, little images of God reflected in the world and in ourselves. It may not be the all of it, but it is a lot. And it is the best we can do.

Question 6

How Can We Reconcile Science with
Belief in God?

I was invited to one of the fourth-grade classes at our day school.
The children had been studying evolution as part of their science
curriculum and the Creation story as part of their Hebrew/Judaica
studies. They wanted to know, "Which one is true?" I think they
were still young enough, or trusting enough, to believe whatever
I could convincingly tell them. Of course, given my position at
the synagogue, they expected me to defend the biblical account.

"If you have a math problem, what kind of book would you
choose to help you?" I queried. "A math book," they all said in
unison. "Exactly. Different books answer different kinds of questions. It may be a good question, but if you look in the wrong
book, you probably will not get the right answer. If you want to
know how the world was created, and how we all came to be a
part of it, you need a science book. Science tries to answer the
"how" question, and one of the possible theories it gives is evolution. A theory means no one is sure; it is a good guess based on
the knowledge we currently have. Lots of things we think are
true are really just theories. Though it may look that way to

those who really do not understand it, the Bible is not trying to answer the "how" question; it wants to answer the "why" question. Why was the world created and why are we a part of it? The Torah's story of creation is not a scientific theory. But you have to read it the right way. Two books, two different questions. You have to know which book to go to when."

One of the defining films of my early teen years was *Inherit the Wind,* based on the Scopes Monkey Trial in Tennessee. The plot centers around a young teacher, fired for teaching evolution in addition to the biblical account of creation. In it, Clarence Darrow, played by Spencer Tracy, was the defense attorney who defeated William Jennings Bryan and made him appear like an ignorant bigot in the process. The film and the play were true products of modernity, a world in which science and progress were pitted against religion and medievalism. It was a pitched battle, but we knew who would be the ultimate winner. Truth could not be held back forever. The Bible and its fictions would have to go. And so they did in the minds of many. If the biblical accounts were not true (i.e., not in accord with scientific "fact"), then the Bible as a whole was unreliable and rather useless.

In the postmodern world in which we live, there need not be winners and losers; rather, as I stated more simply to the fourth graders that day, we can recognize parallel truths that are not in conflict one with the other. Genesis is not science or history, nor does it pretend to be. It is myth. Myths are not lies. Rather, they are stories that teach ultimate truths about the world and human nature. Every society known to humankind has used myths and sacred stories to pass down its values. The biblical account of creation teaches us that there is order in the universe, that creation is good, that we human beings have the responsibility of steward-ship, and that the energy we call God is part and parcel of the totality of all things. These are the real truths of the biblical account. I believe they can stand, side by side, with scientific truths and theories. Though some people in both camps want us to choose sides, my sense is that belief in one does not exclude belief in the other. One can be both a scientist and a person of faith. They are not mutually exclusive. In fact, one of the greatest scientific minds of all time, Albert Einstein, was a very spiritual person. When I read books on physics or mathematics theory, I often feel the affinity these disciplines have with religion.

Furthermore, as Professor Arnie Eisen points out, "The progression from energy to matter to organic life [the Bible's six days of creation] has proven wonderfully suggestive." So has the biblical notion that sea life appeared before land animals. That is to say, while it does not posit itself as science, there are, on occasion, scientific insights or intuitions in the Bible that were based on keen observation of the surroundings. After all, the people who wrote the Bible did not have all the distractions that we have today. They lived in nature, depended upon it, and often understood it in ways that we modern urban dwellers fail to appreciate.

Taking this a step further, I would venture to say that just as we all need science to help us build a better world, science needs religion to rein in its capabilities by providing the moral challenge, the moral questions. Stated another way, it is the role of science to figure out whether or not something *can* be done. And since this task is often driven by the marketplace, science increasingly finds a way to make things happen when people or industry wants them to happen. Only religion, because its moral code is not dependent on what we want, can answer the question "*Ought* it to be done?" As we have seen in our own time, science often begins with a lofty goal but winds up creating a Frankenstein. Religion, because it is a value system, because it responds to a Higher Authority, can dialogue with science on whether or not it is a good idea. Though there are many differing religious points of view, I think the dialogue is both healthy and necessary. I hope we will see lots more of it as time goes on.

Question 7

Does God Have a Plan for Each of Us?

Does God Care About Us on an Individual Level?

Does God Intervene in Our Lives?

Judaism is predicated on choice. From the very first story in the Garden of Eden to Moses' last exhortations on the west bank of the Jordan River, it is clear that we as human beings have been created with free will. Our lives are not programmed like the computer on which I typed these words that you are now reading. We are free to make our own decisions, to follow our own path, to create the very path we will follow.

But does that mean God has no will for us? What about the many interventions we read about in the Bible? Didn't God tell Abraham and Sarah, after offering them the covenant that would change their lives and the course of human history, that their people would be slaves in Egypt for four hundred years? Doesn't God "harden Pharaoh's heart" so that he will not let us leave? And doesn't God then reach down with a "mighty hand and an outstretched arm" to free us from our bondage? If God both knows and directs the course of human history, can we really say that we have free will?

It gets a little more complicated. If God does not know the

outcome in advance, does that mean there are limits to the Divine knowledge, that God is not fully omniscient? And if human beings are free to make their own choices, even to choose evil, does that mean that God is also free to make choices that may go against nature or our sense of justice? Or does God have limits that even we do not?

These are not new questions. Our sages have wrestled with them over the last three millennia. The good news is that there is no one Jewish dogma or creed that has to be believed by all of us. The bad news is that there is no one Jewish dogma or creed for all of us to believe in. Jewish thinking on this subject ranges across the full spectrum of possibilities, influenced, I guess, by experience, personality, and individual belief. There have been Jewish sages who felt all things were predestined—"Everything is determined except the fear of Heaven." And others who held to radical autonomy and free will. While we might want to know what the real truth is, we are definitely free to stake a claim on our own belief. That much freedom I know we have.

Personally, I think the answer is "yes and no." That is not a cop-out, rather, it is a typical Jewish response to much of life. Judaism likes to see things as dialectic, likes to see the other side. It is what I call the tension of the middle. Though we may generally hold to one side *or* the other, either side can be true given a particular set of circumstances. Our beliefs and opinions do change from time to time. Alternatively, the answer may lie somewhere in the middle of both sides. We need the dialectic in order to create the middle ground. If we did not have two sides, there would be no middle; and since the truth is there, in that middle space, we have to be thankful for the opposing point of view.

Years ago I was a high school teacher and the coach of the boys' high school soccer team. I used to say to my players, "Your opponents are not your enemy. They make the game possible. So take good care of them. Make sure they do not get injured by your actions. Play to win, for that is the goal of the game, but play with love and respect." The coaches of the other teams did not quite see it that way, but they did get curious when we won the division title.

I do believe in a God who personally knows and cares for me, who is guiding and shaping the course of my life, who is there for me every single moment, protecting me, watching over me, involved in the most intimate of ways in the details of my existence, and who listens to and is moved by my prayers. The prophet Joel contended that God needs to be roused by our petition and that because of our relationship we have the power to do just that. At the same time, I do not believe that God is a micro-manager. I am responsible for my thoughts, and especially my actions. God does not make me strike out in my softball game nor does the Lord guide my swing when I hit that home run to win the game. Contradiction? I concede that it might be. I am not sure how any of this works, but the older I get, the less I need to know. I feel it as a reality in my life, especially as I look back on it. Those experiences that seemed unrelated or painful or "unnecessary" now seem to have been part of a pattern that led me to this very moment in time. How carefully crafted it all looks from the perspective of time. Perhaps this is the only way we can see God at work—from a distance, kind of like a landscape. We do not know what it looks like from our position on the ground. But go up on a hill that overlooks it, and it reveals itself to us. I believe we can see God at work in our lives (usually) only by looking backward.

God works with us and through us, and through nature as well. When God says, "I have seen the sufferings of My people, have heard their anguished cry, and now will save them," the Lord sends Moses to arrange for their freedom (Exodus 3:7–8, 10). Why not do the deed alone? God does not go down and yank the people out. The hand of God does not reach down from the heavens. There is no hand. We are the hand. God cannot take the people out of Egypt by Himself. That is not the way God works in this world. God wills the people out. We become God's hand by fulfilling that will. In that sense, then, God brought us out of Egypt. It would never have happened without God's will to make it so, but God did not literally take the people out. Moses did. And I was the one who hit that home run, though I suppose we could say that the eye-hand coordination to do so was God's gift. So was the wind blowing out in left field that evening.

There is also our inner voice, the voice of conscience, what the prophet Elisha called, "the still small voice within," the voice that leads us through tough times, that helps us make the right choice. Perhaps that voice is the sum total of all that has been taught us. But sometimes it feels that the whole is greater than all its parts and that this voice has a source wiser than anything I could have known. I am comfortable calling that source God.

God's intervention, then, is real but not actual. God acts through nature, through human beings, through all sorts of ways. We are free to act in accordance with God's will or to reject it and act on our own. God, of course, wants us to act in consonance with the will that is always being revealed to us. Being human, we do not always hear that. Sometimes—lots of times—we are blind to God's reality. Even when we listen we do not always get it or get all of it. Rabbi Lawrence Kushner tells this story of two Jews at the back of the line when the People of Israel crossed the Sea of Reeds. They were looking down, cursing the mud and gunk that was getting on the new sandals they had bought for the trip to the Land of Promise. The entire way, they complained without ceasing about the muddy path Moses had led them on, and so they missed the miracle.

How many of us are looking down, missing God's intervention in our lives right at this moment? Do you really think you would be reading this book if God did not want it to be so? That you woke up this morning, that you will eat food and drink fresh water, that your heart beats and your mind thinks, that your feet stand firmly on an orb spinning on its axis and around the sun at speeds that ought to send you hurtling into space but do not—is any of this possible without the will of God? God's will is made manifest through the laws of nature, and through the laws revealed to us on a mountaintop called Sinai, and through the voice of conscience that cannot be muted, and by the revelation that continues each and every day if we but pay attention long enough to hear it and sense it.

God has a plan for us. I cannot prove that, but I know it is so. Each and every one of us was placed on this planet to complete and fulfill a particular mission or task. The most important thing we can do with our lives is to discover that mission and attempt to fulfill it. Many people I have met think that their profession is their mission, but a job is only a tool, an opportunity; it can never be a mission in and of itself. What we call our potential is none other than God's plan, or will, for us. Again, we can ignore or deny that, as so many do. Theirs are lives of incompleteness and lack of fulfillment, regardless of the material trappings they may acquire—money, fame, power, possessions. As one who ministers to the so-called fortunate members of our society, I urge you to take my word for it: There is a lot of pain and sadness inside those walled-in, security-gated houses. That which comes from outside the self can never bring inner peace and personal fulfillment. It never does. It may look good from the outside. It may even feel good for a moment in time. But it does not last.

Or, we can turn our lives into a search for mission. And when we find it, we can do our best to live that mission in every task and undertaking of our lives. Those who live in this way can never be shaken, despite the bumps and turns in the road. For they have made their way and God's will for them one and the same. This is the true goal of the religious path—to be in sync with God's will. By attempting to stay on that path, we do exactly that.

Question 8
~

What Is the Relationship Between Organized Religion and God? Why Are There So Many Religions? Do We All Worship Different Gods?

Be very quiet. Tune out all the outside noises—the buzzing of lights, the sounds of the street, the whirring of the refrigerator, even the birds chirping. What do you hear? Your breathing. God can be a breath, our breath, the breath of life, each breath we take, you and I, and everyone everywhere—the old woman down the street, that baby in Africa, those children playing the games of youth.

God comes to Moses as YHVH (the Hebrew letters *yud, hey, vav, hey*). In English, this is usually translated as "Lord." Those modern Bibles that are trying to maintain the authenticity of the Hebrew language often use Adonai or lately, Yahweh. While these attempts are better, they still do not adequately express the Hebrew. The name that God uses for the revelation to Moses is made up of four vowels. Try that in English. Can you say "aeiu"? A vowel is meant to be able to pronounce a consonant. But four vowels together? Say it out loud. Not as four separate letters but as a word. All you hear is a whisper. All you hear is your breath. The previous generations did not get that. To them, God ap-

peared as *El Shaddai* God Almighty, a powerful God, one that could
help rid them of their idols and their images. This name, YHVH,
God saved for Moses. What does that tell us about our own God
awareness and consciousness? That God can be different to every one
of us, revealed to different people in different ways. Like us, God
has many names and many aspects of personality. We are not identical in every situation; we do not behave the same way with every
relationship. I explain the same event differently depending on
whether I am telling it to my children or my wife. And, of course,
no two people ever perceive us exactly the same way.

In yoga they say, "Many paths. One God." My children, like
all children, attempt to compare themselves to other kids, especially when they want something that their friends are getting. I
remind them of their uniqueness and tell them I will not be
guided by what others do. In that, I am consistent. Would a
loving parent treat all her children the same way? Like a loving
parent, knowing our limits and our proclivities, our needs and
our abilities, God treats each of us differently. And so it is with
the religions of the world. Each religion represents another child,
another family, another way to approach the One. As there is only
one God, all religions (and all people) are merely manifestations of
the One. The particularities are more human than divine. Each
religion is refracted light. Some colors will be more appealing
than others. With some you will resonate; others may cause you
some discomfort. Even within each hue there will be shades (i.e.,
rituals, dogmas, theologies, customs) that will have various levels
of appeal. It is only out of great love for us that God provides
or allows for all these different ways of relationship, all these ways
for our getting close. The important thing is to find one and
stick to it. That is how we really get close to God.

Tonight, when I go home, I will not go to my neighbor's
house. My neighbor has a good house, with a wonderful wife and
two lovely children. Like us, they are hardworking, successful in
business, contributing members of the community. Still, I will

go to my house. My home is not any better, just different. And it is mine. What is true of my personal home is equally true of my communal home—the synagogue, and the Judaism that stems from its walls. Judaism is one way, not the only way, to live a life with God. How cruel, how unkind and unjust would God be if the Holy One said this was the only path to relationship and connection! I simply do not believe in a God like that. Yes, there are certain general principles. Yes, there are universal rules. But only one name, only one prayer book written in one ancient language, only one set of stories, one sacred Bible, one set of folkways and customs? That is not the God I know.

The recognition of this truth was part and parcel of the development of human consciousness and culture. Originally, people worshiped many gods. There was a god of the sun and a god of the earth, a god for fertility, a god for rain, good gods and evil ones. Seafaring people had a god of the seas, and warmongers had a god that followed them into battle. With the advent of Judaism, beginning with Abraham and Sarah, a shift occurred. Judaism posited the possibility that an individual could have only one God in spite of the fact that many gods existed. In other words, Abraham and Sarah were not monotheists in the strict sense of the word. They owned the fact that other gods existed, but they were in a faithful covenant with only one of them—Adonai. It was kind of like a monogamous marriage. We know there are other men and women out there. We may look once in a while, but we do not sleep with them. This helps us understand the biblical use of the term "jealous" when it comes to the God of the Hebrews. If there was only one God, there would be nothing to be jealous about. It is only because the ancient Hebrews kept looking to other gods for their needs that God could be jealous regarding their behavior.

Even in the time of Moses, strict monotheism was not in force. When he says to the children of Israel, *Sh'mah Yis-rah-ale, Ah-doe-nigh Eh-lo-hay-noo, Ah-doe-nigh eh-chahd*, which is usually translated as, "Hear, O Israel, the Lord is our God, the Lord is One," I think he meant something else. Look at the context of his statement (Deuteronomy 6). I believe Moses is saying, "Listen up, Israel, Adonai is our God, and only Adonai." He was reminding them of their covenant of faithfulness, which had been broken by the previous generation's (understandable) fixation on the gods of Egypt. It was not until much later in human history (the time from which the accepted translation derives) that the notion of there really being only one God who unites us all as a single family on earth came to be accepted. I wholeheartedly endorse that idea because of what it teaches us—that all people everywhere, everyone who ever was or ever will be, are connected by the same Creator. As a result, no one can say, "My God is better than your God; my religion is superior to yours." We are all truly brothers and sisters, children of the One.

Why so many religions, then? Why can't we all agree on one universal religion and stop all the fighting between Christians and Protestants, Muslims and Jews, Hindus and Muslims, and so on? Why so many families? Why so many homes? Tonight, why don't you go to your neighbor's house and sleep in her bed instead of your own? Isn't it just as good as yours, maybe even better? Our humanity is expressed in particularity. We are not any person. Each of us is a particular person. And though we share in universal truths and commonalities, we experience them through our unique and particular personhood. Someday it might be otherwise. Someday there will be no divisions and no differences. But in the meantime, the best we can do is provide a loving embrace to all people, making our houses of worship places where everyone can come and feel welcome. Of course, there are also historical, political, and economic factors that have led to the development of different religions. We would be naïve to think otherwise. Since this is a book of theology, however, I will simply acknowledge those other factors and allow others to explain them more fully.

While we share certain universalistic features, it is in the very nature of human beings to be particular individuals. After all, what is a body, a name, an identity, a family? They are limits. They are ways of defining me as an individual—this person and not someone else. That does not make me any better than anyone else, just different. As it is with me, so it is with the extensions of myself—my family, my country, my profession, my religion. All of these help me to self-define and to define myself to others. Part of the human condition is making these decisions, these explorations of self. Coming to terms with who and what you are is part of the growth process of every human being.

At the same time, I recognize that I am not just this person. In fact, one might say that this particularism is an illusion. In truth, I consist of molecules, water and air or space, the same things that constitute you and everyone else. Religion teaches us that beyond this material self is an eternal soul that comes from God, also shared by all people everywhere. This soul, since it is eternal, is my real self. Terry Bookman is just a temporary blip on the screen of existence. I am a soul. You are a soul. And all that is, is God. We are all part of the One. We are all one.

It is somewhat ironic that religion takes the form of particularity to teach us universal truths. But no more ironic than me taking human form to learn this about myself. In the end, we are stuck with our limitation. But it is only through that limitation that I can know my limitlessness. We become conscious of the universal through our particularity. There is no other way. And even if we created just one religion, and forced everyone into it, that, too, would be its own particularism. There is just no getting around this reality.

The purpose of religion, then, its true purpose, is to teach us that we are all one. It does so with different means, sounds, smells, customs, rituals—all these are teaching tools, getting our attention and keeping us interested. That there are many choices is a good thing. What kind of ice cream store would offer only vanilla? That I learn to tolerate those differences—this needs to be taught by every faith tradition. That I choose the way of my ancestors, my family—this is natural for many and impossible for others. Some people just never relate to the faith of their birth family. They feel as if they were born into the wrong body. They suffer, feel incomplete. Some let it go without a thorough, adult investigation, which is too bad. Though it may hurt when one of our children forsakes the "family" for another religion, we need to grow through our pain and personal disappointment to recognize they are still on the path to the One. Then we may share the commonalities that unite us, while learning to accept and be challenged by the nuances of difference that may yet enhance our own journeys.

Part Two

Pathways to God

Introduction

～

Though the cliché states "Seeing is believing," the truth is that the witnessing of miracles or even direct encounters do not create a faith that is unshakable. They do not help us to sense the presence of God all the time. Our very humanity does not allow that to happen. We forget. We deny the reality. We turn our attention toward ourselves and the people/things of our world, and we fail to recognize the primary reality of our lives, of life itself. We are all so busy, doing and acquiring, building our lives and our careers, making a name for ourselves, seeking fulfillment (often in all the wrong places), running away from pain, or just trying to hold it all together. Modernity was going to make it easy for us. But, we have found out it isn't so easy.

And, then, we realize we are broken. Each of us, just because we are human, is a flawed vessel, cracked and wounded by life experience. You and me, all of us, trying to pretend that we are not, that we have it all together. Smiling in spite of the fear and the pain. Hiding. We cannot hold all that is poured into us. That is just the way it is. There is no perfection. God is present at every moment, in every space (where can we go that God is not?), but we are unable to stay conscious of that reality for any length of time. This is our imperfection. The limits of our humanity. We get it, but we forget.

Many of us have had this notion that the spiritual should just come to us. I call this "oh wow! spirituality." If you are open to the possibility and you really want it, then it should happen. Especially if you are an essentially nice person. But it does not happen that way. At least not for me. No more than I can stay in shape without working out or dieting. Each day I have to confront that treadmill, or bicycle, put on those gym shoes, and say no to that delicious piece of high-fat whatever, all in an effort to control my weight and keep those arteries unblocked. It's work!

Judaism teaches us that to stay God-conscious is also work. It takes discipline and repeated effort and will, just like working out or dieting does. Yes, there are people who can eat like a pig and never gain an ounce—I am not one of them. Similarly, there are some people who seem to have an awareness of or a relationship with God that is natural and present all the time, with no effort on their part. Perhaps they have been chosen by God. Or perhaps they are the spiritual Beethovens of our world—simply born with "it." And there are even more of us who have a moment in which God is real—driving home from work on that familiar street, skiing down a hill, birthing our children. For some, these moments are enough; these folks seek no more. The moments are sustaining. And there are still others for whom such moments are so frightening, so upsetting of their world, that consciously or unconsciously, they close themselves off to the possibility of more. They are satisfied with their lives—or at least they say they are. But for those who want more, us God junkies, we will have to work for it. We have no choice.

Using Your Head

Our tradition offers us three basic paths to do this work, and each path represents a certain proclivity or personality type. One path is that of the *hacham*, or intellectual, and that is the path of study. In Judaism, the intellectual pursuit of God is also a spiritual endeavor. We can reach God through our heads. This is the person who wants to know, who hungers after knowledge, who is willing to pursue the truth wherever it may be found. While the content of the search may be important, it is the search itself that is the substance of this path. And so the seeker could be a scientist trying to develop a cure for a disease or a theory of the universe. Or she could be a historian piecing together the fragments of a little-known event. Or they could be the members of my Torah study group, looking for personal meaning in those same old stories we read last year. Writers, theologians, philosophers, kitchen table debaters—people who live in the world of ideas—all may be on the path of the *hacham*.

When I sit with an ancient text, I feel the presence of those who came before me, who also pored over its words. They sat in candlelit rooms or hid in caves. Some risked imprisonment or even death. Others were as comfortable as I, at my table, pen in mouth, just in case an idea comes to me while I'm reading. I have written two theses in my life, for two different degrees. In each case, my research had to be original. I had to say things that no one else had ever said before. I spent days on each point, analyzing the possibilities in my head. I remember the feeling, though I am certain that words will never express it entirely. It felt as if I was standing on a precipice, my feet unsteady, my destination unclear, my ability to ever "get there" uncertain. What did I want to say? What was the message, the secret locked inside the hundreds of handwritten notes to myself? Could I hold it all together? Could I birth these words, this new creation? How? How would I ever get there?

This search into the abyss of truth, understanding, knowledge, and wisdom is a way of entering the mind of God, of being in the presence, of touching the mystery and cracking it for a little while, only to realize before long that the curtains have been drawn once again. But the *hacham* will not be deterred. Soon a new project will call, a new thought will compel, another text will beg for attention. Or perhaps it will be yet another new angle on an old idea. It matters little. For the *hacham*, the path is the pursuit. Truth is the goal, measured in little drops along the way.

Following Your Heart

A second path is that of the *navi*, or prophet, and that is the path of direct communication or prayer. We can also reach God through our hearts. At one time, in the ancient world, our people were led by such types. They were called "prophets," and they claimed that God spoke directly to them. "Thus says the Lord" was a familiar introduction to a longer speech that indicated our responsibilities to the One. And then the age of prophecy was deemed to have ended. We no longer listened to those who spoke to God. Prayer became a more directed experience, communal, ordered, and rote.

But the need to communicate directly with the Divine did not end. Nor did this personality type disappear. Some *navi'im* (the plural of *navi*) seem to have a fire in the bones. Their awareness of being in the presence of God is immediate and continuously present. They speak to God as one speaks to a friend. It is natural and normal. Since Judaism was profoundly shaped by the words of prophets, perhaps it is ironic that I find this type present much more often among faithful Christians. The ability simply to speak forth prayers at a given moment, no matter what the occasion, no matter what the situation, is theirs. I am running around looking for a prayer book, and they are just talking to God.

I met a couple once whose son was the first Jewish kid on his football team in a small Indiana town. School prayer issues aside, this coach always began the games with his team kneeling in prayer. Being very ecumenical and wanting to be fair, he asked this Jewish kid to lead them in prayer for the first game of the season. With the stares of all his teammates upon him, he closed his eyes and said, "*Bah-rooch Ah-tah Ah-doe-nigh Eh-lo-hay-noo meh-lech ha-o-lahm, ha-mo-tzee leh-chem meen ha-ah-retz,* Yeah!" The team clapped their hands and went out and won the game. So the prayer was repeated each week through an undefeated season, the players never knowing that they were blessing bread, the only prayer the kid knew by heart. Jews seem to have lost the ability to simply speak unself-consciously to God.

For most non-Orthodox Jews, with the exception of the High Holy Days, attending a worship service has become an event, an activity they do when invited or compelled by someone who is "up on the *bimah*"—their child reading a prayer, a couple being blessed, a baby being named, a friend receiving an honor. They are not really there to pray, but if the service is good, or the cantor's voice appeals, they can and do find themselves carried into the worship. Others are what I call "minyanaires," the ones who are always there at services. The minyanaires are there to pray. They know the liturgy from childhood memory, or because they were in the adult B'nai Mitzvah class and got turned on. They are there each week to connect to self, to others, even to God. It is the communal nature of the experience that adds incentive for them to show up each week. They would be missed if they were not there, and they know it.

More and more, in the Jewish world, small minyanim/prayer groups (literally, "quorum," which has been defined as ten people, the minimum number we need to elicit a sense of community) are being formed to respond to this need. They are often an alternative to the regular worship service in the sanctuary, less formal, more experimental and creative, more personal, lay-led (at least in part), and interactive. In some synagogues, several of these go on at once for different special-interest groups—a singles minyan, a learners' minyan, a meditation minyan, an all-women minyan, a youth one, one geared for preschoolers, and the like. We are returning to modalities once forgotten in the Jewish community. Group singing, *niggunim* (melodies without words), extended silence, personal prayers for healing, movement, percussion instruments and hand clapping. We are experiencing prayer as a joyous expression of the heart, one that is uplifting and inspiring, one that has us seeking more. And one that has us creating that which has been missing in our modern world—a genuine sense of community and belonging.

Just Doing It

The third path is that of the *hasid*/pious one (not to be confused with the contemporary expression of religious observance known as Hasidism). This is the person who is a doer, doing for others, visiting them in hospitals, celebrating their *simchas* (joyous occasions), comforting them in time of sorrow, feeding them in food pantries and homeless shelters, leading the clothing drive, volunteering time and effort, giving and raising money for *tzedakah* (literally righteous action), being foster parents or adopting orphaned children. This may also be the person who is involved in taking care of our planet, recycling, saving endangered species, adopting stray animals, growing a natural garden, and using organic fertilizers. They take care of others and our world as an expression of their commitment to God (even if they do not always use that word), for they see all of creation as God's gift to us. We are renters in this world, not owners. It is our task to be caretakers and to pass it on to the next generation.

The true *hasid* looks to be involved in simple and profound acts of love and kindness.

We all know people like that. The ones who are always there, no matter what the need. Some do so just because it is the right thing to do. Most cannot articulate it, which is probably why they are drawn to this path in the first place. Don't call them to do the planning or attend the meetings. But when it comes time to work, they will be first. My son Jonah is like that. Serving food at the shelter, he greets each person with a smile and a story. Shaking hands, carrying a mother's tray so she can carry her child, wiping up spills, finding something extra for anyone who asks. Then he goes home and cries at the injustice of it all. If the *hacham* uses her brain, and the *navi* his heart, then the path of the *hasid* is through the hands and the feet. We could say they are the hands and feet of God in this world, God's true partners, God's helpers.

Opening the Soul

To these classic three, I would add a fourth—the path of the *ohev,* the lover, the one who finds God in and through relationship with others and with life itself. While I have written in other places that soul is not a separate entity in Judaism, rather it is reached through everyday actions and awareness, I would risk contradicting myself by venturing that this fourth path is the path of the soul. Yes, relationships could be understood through any of the other paths. Who could deny that relating to another human being requires heart (communicating), head (understanding), hands and feet (doing)? But relationships cannot be neatly confined to these alone. For what is a relationship, what is true love if not the opening of our soul to the other? Herein lies the mystery and the power of loving another human being. We connect to that ineffable part of the other and become one.

Such awareness is experienced by many in the so-called falling-in-love stage. It is as if we have lost our own identity and are merging with the other. We fail to delineate where one of us begins and the other ends. But it is also the love of parents and children, true friends, siblings; it is the love that a teacher has for students; a physician for patients; the "master" for disciples; a rabbi or minister for congregants; it can even be experienced within the realm of nature and things. It is a love that can arise in an instant, but more likely after many years of being with and caring for the other. It is a love that has no possessiveness; rather, it seeks only the growth, well-being, and wholeness of the other. Many of us confuse it with the sexual encounter. While there are certainly features in common, sex does not automatically equal love or relationship. In fact, sometimes sex can mask and obstruct the true love that can and ought to exist.

The *ohev* is passionate about life, admires beauty, seeks pleasure within acceptable limits, enjoys food and art and music, feels at home in nature, surrounds himself or herself with aesthetic environments—seeing all of this as God's creation. In the Talmud we are told that when we arrive at the gates of heaven we will be asked only one question: "Why did you not partake of the pleasures that were permitted to you in the land of the living?" The *ohev* will have no trouble answering that question. She or he will simply reply, "But I did. I did."

Some of us are eclectic by nature, and so there can be hybrids of all these paths. There is even one type who tries to be equally balanced in all of them. That is what I call the *tzaddik*/righteous one. It is the path that I have attempted to travel most of my adult life. Perhaps that is why I chose to be a congregational rabbi (though sometimes it feels as if it chose me). We are professional mitzvah doers. It is our "job" to study, pray, and do for others. Judaism purports that we can find God, connect to God, make God a presence in our life by consistent conscious action in any or all of these paths. Through studying, praying, and/or doing for others—take your pick—one may live a life with God as partner. This is what we call true "mitzvah," actions or thoughts that keep us close to God. Of course, they must be done with that awareness, lest they become disconnected positive acts (at best) or "religious behaviorism" (at worst), repeated and mindless actions that may actually cause more harm than good. We all know such people as well. They appear to be religious, but their hearts are bitter, angry, and resentful. Far from bringing them closer to God, their behavior damages them and those around them, turning them off or away from God.

So which is the best path? Which does Judaism value the most? The truth is, we need to encourage all the paths, for each of us is different. Each of us has proclivities that will lead us to one path or the other. Proclivity does not mean choice or will; rather, it denotes that to which we are drawn. Our spiritual type, if you will. The world needs all of these energies, all of these types, to maintain its wholeness and balance.

Some of us are naturally intellectual; others cannot even pick up a book. Some can pray with fluidity and love the ambience and aesthetics of the synagogue; others do not have the heart for prayer and are easily bored by worship. Those who are gifted to study are not better (or worse) than those who visit the sick. One who is blocked in interpersonal relationships may still serve others through his or her profession or by working for social justice. I like the fact that Judaism recognizes different ways of getting there, when the "there" is God. One path is not more spiritual than the others. All paths are equally valid ways of connecting to God. Besides, since we are continually evolving and changing, the path we choose today may very well be different from the path we will travel tomorrow. How many times have I seen the birth of a child, or a tragedy, or retirement from one's occupation set a person on a brand-new journey! What we reject at one stage in our lives may very well become the substance of another moment in time.

The Path of the Heart:

Prayer

President Clinton visits Benjamin Netanyahu in Jerusalem. He walks into his office and sees several telephones. A blue one is the direct line to the White House; a red one to the Kremlin. Then there is a white one. Clinton asks, "What is this one?" Netanyahu smiles and responds, "Oh, that one is to God." "To God?! May I try it?" "Why not? Just dial the number one." So Clinton presses "one," and sure enough, he is talking to God. He is so impressed that he asks Netanyahu where he can get such a phone. The prime minister simply gives him that one, saying he has plenty. The president is back in the White House maybe five minutes when he plugs in his new white phone and presses "one." An operator comes on the line and says, "That will be fifteen dollars for the first three minutes." Confused, Clinton replies, "But I just called a few days ago, and it was free." "Free? From where did you place that call, sir?" "From Jerusalem." "Well, sir, from there it is a local call."

Call it chutzpah, maybe, but Jews have always felt a direct access to God. Only our telephone line for the last two thousand years has been prayer. Prayer, not as some special event for which we get dressed up and go to a synagogue where we feel uncomfortable, incompetent, and out of place, to be led by a rabbi and cantor through words and rituals we do not understand, but prayer as simple, straightforward conversation, prayer as communication. Prayer as a time-out from the everyday and the practical, from our incessant running to get something done, to be productive, active, successful. Prayer in which we address God in the informal *Ah-tah,* like the French *tu,* the intimate pronoun we use when we know and love the other.

And yet it seems so few of us really pray with any regularity anymore. Oh, I know the excuses we use; I have heard them all—too much Hebrew, takes too long, like the old "traditional" melodies better, rabbi is boring, don't like the cantor's voice, am not religious, too tired at the end of the week, the service times don't work with my schedule, don't have kids at home anymore, have kids at home and don't get to see them, too many other things going on in my life right now, not sure if I even believe in God. Have I left any out?

The Hebrew word for prayer is *l'hitpallel* (pronounced l'heet-pah-layle). It is in the grammatical category of reflexive verbs; that is to say, it represents a type of action that is done within oneself, or to oneself. Prayer, then, as understood in the Jewish tradition, is a type of internal dialogue that we whisper, or say out loud. It is a conversation we have within ourselves. We can use this conversation as a kind of time-out from the craziness of our lives in which we pause to seek clarity, to connect with self and others, to work on our particular issues, to talk things over with God. In the Jewish tradition, then, totally silent prayer is really an oxymoron.

Our tradition holds out the possibility that the spirituality we seek, that sense of connection to self and to the Transcendent, is available to us through prayer. Perhaps not all the time, perhaps not every time we pray, but lots of times. Sometimes we may feel that connection to the person sitting next to us; sometimes to that person whose name we cannot remember but whom we recognize from across the sanctuary; sometimes to those young parents vainly trying to keep their toddler amused so they can grab a few minutes of prayer time; and sometimes to life itself as the sunlight shines through the window or the stained glass upon our face. We pray every day to make possible a context in which we will have moments of connection.

I liken a Jewish worship service to a play in four acts. We have all been to the theater. We know what that experience is all about. A play is meant to take us away for a little while, to lift us up, to challenge our thinking, to entertain, to help us reexamine what is most important in our lives. But in order for that to happen, we have to suspend our disbelief. We have to let go of the stuff of our everyday lives—the problems at the office, the meeting we must attend the next day, the argument over dinner—and pretend that the actors up on the stage are really the people they are pretending to be. If they remain in our minds as actors playing a role, nothing will occur for us. We will have wasted a couple of hours sitting around. The lights, the curtain, the music, as well as the power of the performance—all are meant to make the experience possible. But in the end, if we block it out by staying stuck in ourselves, it will not matter how great the play really was.

Prayer works much the same way. The actors are replaced by prayer leaders whose task it is to create an environment in which we can let go of whatever realities or baggage we were carrying when we entered the worship space, so that we can be lifted up and out of ourselves. In this there is real transformation, sometimes momentary, sometimes partial, and sometimes—just sometimes—permanent and ultimate. That is the goal of prayer. It is a shift from our self-consciousness to self-surrender, in which we realize we are not the center of the universe around which everything must revolve; rather, God is. Praying is not about attending services; it is about giving of ourselves and giving of our time to God. To deepen us, widen us, make us bigger than we were. To take us from where we were, wherever that happens to be, and move us, one step at a time, to where we might yet be. How big a step? Well, that will depend on our willingness, our openness, our capacity to move.

Praying Alone Versus Praying in Synagogue

One of the questions I am most frequently asked on the topic of prayer is, "Why do I have to pray in synagogue? Why can't I just pray on my own?" And my answer is, "You do not have to pray in synagogue. You can pray anywhere at any time, by yourself or with others. There is nothing inherently more holy about a prayer spoken in the sanctuary than a prayer spoken in your car, on the treadmill, in your living room, or out in nature on your morning walk." I believe God listens to all our prayers, regardless of when they are spoken and by whom. I often pray by myself, mixing my prayers with meditation and chanting. Given the realities of my life and the schedule choices I make, without private prayer I would not have much of a prayer life.

Why bother praying in synagogue, then? Especially when it is often inconvenient or inaccessible, even distracting? While I believe we are being honest when we say we pray on our own, the trouble is, being human, we will often not pray unless we have a community of others with whom we do so. I mean, that is why groups like Weight Watchers have been so successful. We could come up with those diets ourselves. But we need the support and encouragement of others. And without it, we will find excuses and convenient rationalizations so that the best of our intentions will soon evaporate.

But it is more than that. Prayer is also a conversation we have with a community of others, which we call "minyan." To be a part of a minyan is to link oneself with a community of "pray-ers," to bind oneself to fixed times of getting together, to declare that you are no longer complete by being totally alone. Soon after my son Ariel's bar mitzvah, nine of us were sitting in the chapel waiting for a tenth so that we could begin our worship service. In he walked and someone said, "Now we are a community. Now we can begin." To be a part of a minyan is to know that you count, that the community is truly diminished by your absence. For some, this is spiritual experience enough.

Minyan is also a type of dance. We dance with the prayer leader called the *shaliach tzibur* (literally, "the representative of the community"), we dance with one another, we dance with God. We dance with words and with melodies, sometimes together, sometimes apart. There is space for us to do our own thing, but there are also times when we are as one. A good minyan provides us with the opportunity to be alone in the context of a group experience. As in any dance, it takes time to learn all the moves and to work together. But when those things happen, it can be a thing of beauty, a work of art.

A minyan ought to be a warm and welcoming place, one in which everyone has the opportunity to get to know one another. I remember leading a workshop for a church group in which I had people sharing their personal beliefs and theologies. In the reflection time at the end, one gentleman said that in all the years he had been attending church services, he had never known anything of significance about the person who sat in front of him week in and week out, singing the same prayers and hymns. He knew when he got a haircut, could describe the hairs on the back of the guy's neck, but he did not know what he felt or thought about anything. I think that is the way it is in many houses of worship. At our synagogue the minyan has become a place in which we share our concerns as well as our joys, a place in which we care for and hold one another in all our vulnerability and fragility. We speak the names of loved ones who are in need of blessing, and we talk about our triumphs big and small. We sing a lot and clap our hands, sometimes we get up and dance, and everyone has a chance to participate, even the newcomer or one of our frequent visitors. In a world of great flux and uncertainty, the minyan has become an island of stability and comfort—and in some immeasurable but nonetheless real way, it makes my communication with God seem more possible.

Prayer Books and Hebrew

I was sitting in the lounge of my kibbutz volunteer house. Having arrived in Israel for the first time only a few days earlier, my knowledge of spoken, modern Hebrew at that point amounted to *shalom*, and perhaps a few other words. I could read the words, *daven* with the best of them, but like most Americans, I did not understand what it was I was saying. In the lounge were people from all over the world—Mexico, Switzerland, France, India, New Zealand, South Africa, and Ethiopia. At least six languages were being spoken in that room, but most of us could not speak to one another. And then someone took out a guitar and started playing Hebrew songs and prayers. Soon the room was filled with singing, and a knowing look came over our faces. Though we came from many different lands, we were united by the Hebrew language.

It was then for the first time, at the age of twenty-eight, that I realized the power of Hebrew. It is the only language that Jews have used for our entire existence. It is the language of our sacred texts and the language of prayer. And even though we can pray in the vernacular, and despite the fact that most Jews cannot even read the words, the use of Hebrew remains for us a very powerful instrument in prayer. In fact, not knowing what the words mean can often be an enhancement to true prayer. We can hear the sounds, feel the centuries of connection, turn off left-brain rational thinking, and allow the words and music to wash over us, to evoke feelings, to travel to a different level of consciousness. This works even when we read the Hebrew in transliteration. And I have been told it works in other traditions as well—Latin Gregorian chanting, Hindu Sanskrit, mantras.

Though some people complain that they are put off by Hebrew because they can't read it or understand it, the real problem in the use of the *siddur*/prayer book is not one of language. It is the problem of rote repetition, mindlessly saying the same prayers over and over again. Jewish tradition calls for both *keval*/fixed prayers (and fixed times for prayer) and *kavanah*/intentionality and spontaneity. It demands both. Fixed prayers are necessary because very few of us are poets. Fixed prayers unite us with other Jews around the world, both past and present. Fixed prayers help us because we don't always have the words with which to pray. And intentionality so that the words are not mere rote repetition and prayer a type of religious behaviorism. We need to say the words with feeling. We need to add something new to our prayers each and every day. And if we cannot, or do not, on some level it may have been better not to have prayed at all.

But how do we say those words with feeling if we don't know what they mean, or worse, don't believe in what the words are saying? Sometimes, knowing what the words mean can diminish their power. Though it was neat when they first started doing it, I know I like opera much better without the subtitles. I can get into it more without the distraction of reading the words, which are often less engaging, less meaningful, even pedantic in comparison with the voices that are singing them. Additionally, we have to remember that the prayer book is not a catechism, not an affirmation of faith. No one is going to take an exit survey to determine if the words you prayed accurately described your faith at that exact moment in time. Our beliefs are continually changing and evolving. A prayer book cannot change that often, nor would we want it to. Besides, we have private prayer to express our personal beliefs. So if you come across a prayer that you find offensive, skip over it, don't say it, hum the melody without the words. No one is keeping score.

An invention that has probably done as much harm as it has good to the worship experience is the printing press. Before the printed *siddur,* the congregation must have known a few prayers by heart, but they had to fill up the prayer time with their private prayers and meditations. When we have a book in front of us, most of us, good students that we are, feel compelled to read and complete it. It feels like cheating if we do not. A quality worship experience is one that allows for a goodly amount of private time, self-paced *davening,* readings and prayers in the margins of the text that allow one to wander within the context of the service. We need to be treated as adults who can find their way into and out of the formal group experience that is being provided by the *shaliach tzibur.* All this in a positive environment that is joyous and upbeat even as it is uplifting.

Once upon a time we owned our own *siddurim* and carried them with us wherever we went. This allowed for a much greater level of privatization because we could write notes in them, or stuff them with alternative readings and prayers. There is nothing like having your own book. It carries a piece of you and your story wherever you go. It becomes a friend. Perhaps that is one reason people like sitting in the exact same seat week after week. Unless the custodians got creative that week, the congregants get to use the same prayer book each time they are there. All they need to do is check the dedication plate inside the front cover— "in memory of" or "in honor of"—and they are all set.

There is a *hasidic* story about a great rabbi who comes to a town whose citizens are renowned for their knowledge of the worship service. Yet when he gets to the entrance of the synagogue, he tells his hosts that he cannot enter. "Why not?" they exclaim. "We have saved you the best seat, next to the eastern wall." "You don't understand," he replies. "The sanctuary is too filled with prayers." As important as they are, the words are not everything. But when we say them with the proper intention, when we allow for the spontaneous strivings of the heart to be expressed, then the prayers rise up to heaven, and there is plenty of space for all who wish to enter.

Types of Prayer

In the mystical tradition of Judaism, the hour of midnight is considered the most propitious time for prayer. Midnight represents the moment in time that is not of this day or of the next. It hangs between time, almost unworldly, and because of that, anything seems possible. As a parent of a new driver (our first), I have come to find new meaning in praying at midnight, that moment in which my internal biological parental clock begins to look for the headlights to shine on the driveway, to listen for the car to pull up, to churn inside at the sound of the phone ringing. Yes, until that boy rapidly growing toward manhood is safe within the confines of our home, midnight has become a time of fervent prayer on my part.

Most of us are familiar with that type of prayer, prayer as a type of asking, of making requests. We want or need something, and so we ask God for it. To this type of prayer we may add two more—prayers in praise of God, and prayers of gratitude for all that we have. Every praying tradition contains these three categories of prayer, and if you look at any prayer book, you will find examples of all three.

Prayer Imagery

One of the consistent prayer problems that people bring to me is that they have trouble praying *to* God. They like coming to services, they enjoy listening to my teaching and sermons (of course), they like the feeling of connection to community past and present that regular attendance brings, but they just cannot get over the process of praying to an "other." On closer examination, I usually find that it is not the process per se that bothers them; rather, it is the image of God as all-knowing, all-powerful king that pervades the *siddur* which they find unsatisfactory, even untenable.

The image of God as king is just that, an image. It is neither sacred nor sacrosanct. It was created at a time when monarchs were the most powerful people known. Since, as Jews, we were not to worship any flesh-and-blood ruler, natural creation, or images of our own making, God was imaged as "King of Kings." (This was paralleled in the Christian tradition, which saw the "kingdom of heaven" as the one true kingdom and the one on earth as almost irrelevant.) Calling God "King" made sense to those people in their day. If it no longer makes sense, we are free to change it, either in print or in our own conceptualization, or both. It is no different for me when I am worshiping in a church. I feel very free to pray in church, but when the name Jesus is used, I simply substitute "God," or "Adonai," or "Lord," or any other name/image for God that comes up at that particular moment. It is only a word, a name we use. We know that in reality God is beyond any name or label. Not that different from us. We are not our names, either.

Yet people are very attached to these images. Even many people who do not like them insist on using them and feel awkward if they do not. After all, we have been using them for centuries. I remember when I was a student in rabbinic school in Los Angeles. Worship services were led by the students, and Wednesdays were creative service days. We could literally do anything we wanted on those days, in the spirit of experimentation and growth. A group of us decided to write an egalitarian service, in Hebrew as well as English. English is easy. One can degender the English language. But Hebrew? We decided to use *both* genders for God in Hebrew, alternating the verbs and pronouns, calling God She as well as He. In retrospect, I don't think the service worked very well. It was awkward and sounded funny; the cadences of the melodies and chants were all off. Nevertheless, it was an interesting attempt for the point we were trying to make. During the evaluation process afterward, however, we were screamed at for "taking the gender issue and the language of the prayer book too seriously, too literally. God is neither male nor female!" "Then why are you screaming at us?" replied one of my coconspirators.

God language is serious, but it ought not be seen as a substitute for the reality of God. We are free to experiment, to call God by many names—Friend, Beloved, Mother/Father, Holy One, Healer, Helper. We can use the names and pronouns handed down by our tradition—King, Rock, Lord of Hosts, Almighty—when those work for us. We may even have different names for God, depending on the nature of the conversation, just as we have different names, some public and others private, for those we love. In fact, the rabbinic tradition, which knew of seventy world languages, boldly declares that there are seventy names for God. In other words, as many as there are peoples. And if praying *to* God is felt to be an impediment, then pray to the God within— "the still, small voice" that the prophet Elisha identified.

Each of us is a filter, which is why God can be different to different people. It is as if God is continually projecting godliness outward. We, having been shaped by the sum total of our experiences, our personalities, our psychological and spiritual makeup, our needs, our life space, our consciousness, will have an awareness or understanding of God that says more about us than it says about the Holy One. As God appears to us, so must our names and images. While this may be difficult to accomplish as a community, with everyone agreeing on the same image, certainly as an individual it is more than possible. You just need to give yourself permission to call on God in your own unique way.

By the way, there are many reasons why one may choose to pray, only one of which is communication with God. Clarification of values, wrestling with important questions, a need to express feelings and concerns, an opportunity to connect with one's community, an effort to help shape experience, the appreciation of the poetry and the music—these are some additional experiences that prayer makes available to us.

Does God Answer All Prayer?

The answer is "Yes." God hears and answers all prayers. The problem is, many of us think that when we ask for something from God and do not get it, it is God who has ignored our pleas. In that conceptualization, God becomes a type of dispensing machine, and when we do not get what we want, we shake the machine, angrily punch the buttons again and again, curse and walk away if nothing comes out.

It is like the story of the drowning man. A man is drowning in the ocean, hanging on to a piece of wood, when a raft comes along. The guy in the raft says, "Jump in," but the man in the water responds, "God will save." Next, a yacht comes along and throws him a lifeline, yelling, "Grab the rope and we'll pull you in." But once again his response is, "God will save." Finally, a helicopter flies overhead. The pilot lowers a rope ladder, shouting, "Grab on and start climbing." And again the response is the same. After that, no other help arrives and so the man drowns. His soul goes to heaven, where he demands an audience with God. He complains to God that his faith and trust were pure, but God let him down. Then it is God's turn. "I don't know what your problem is. I sent you a raft, a yacht, and a helicopter. After that, I gave up on you."

God answers our prayers, sometimes directly and sometimes through an emissary (in Hebrew, *malach*, usually translated as "angel"); sometimes giving us what we need, even if it is not what we want. And sometimes God's answer is "No." "No" is an answer. My children hear it quite often. "No" can be a very loving word. In fact, at times it is the most loving word we can say, like when they want to do something that we perceive can be harmful or dangerous to them. They may not like to hear it. They may even ask again, feeling as though I did not respond. I will then have to remind them that I already answered their question, and the answer is "No." Then they try their luck with their mother. When we do not get the answer we want, sometimes we feel unheard, not listened to. This is one aspect of our human condition and our fragility.

When it comes to God, we are encouraged to ask, ask for everything and anything. The prophet Joel reminds us that sometimes God has to be roused by our petitions, but that we have the power to do so. Pour out your heart to God. There is nothing we can say that could have an adverse effect on our relationship. God will love us just the same. "God, I want a new bicycle . . . help me pass that test . . . make my mother well again . . . let me be the hero of the game." Asking is a way of dumping out, a way of identifying our real needs, separating them from our desires. If we get into the praxis of asking, eventually we will ask God for fewer and fewer things, recognize that we already receive so much even without asking, and take control of that which is in our power to control. This is the path to spiritual maturity.

God listens. God hears. How could it be otherwise? What could we possibly say or think that God would not be able to hear? And if we get quiet enough, if we block out all the noise that is so much a part of our lives (like tuning in that old-fashioned radio), we may even hear what God has to say to us. For every prayer, there is also an answer—not always the one we want to hear, but an answer nevertheless. Our ability to hear it depends on our willingness to listen as well as our capacity for acceptance. We may also need a little patience. Some questions are more difficult than others. We may have to ask them again and again. If it is an important enough question, we will do just that, no matter how long it takes.

Another way God speaks to us is through the words of the Torah. I do not mean that the Torah is literally the word of God, though some people do believe this. But if after we have truly opened our hearts in prayer to God, we listen to the Torah reading as God's "talk back" section, we may just be able to hear God's word for us, sometimes responding to a question that we have asked, and sometimes to the one we do not know how to ask. Think about that the next time you are at a bar or bat mitzvah service—listen to God's word through the voice of a child embarking on the path to adulthood. At our synagogue we have a large and ever growing Torah Corps, laypeople capable of reading/ chanting the Torah. God's voice, then, has become many voices— women who were denied the opportunity when they were adolescents, men, Jews by choice, young and old seeking to deepen their sense of Jewish authenticity. It is perhaps what the rabbis meant when they said that at Sinai we each heard the Torah through the voices of our parents, no two exactly alike.

Barriers and Distractions: Letting Go

It is a well-known adage in the spiritual disciplines of all faiths that as soon as we begin to make some progress in our prayer life, we will begin to run into all kinds of stumbling blocks that will attempt to knock us off our course. In some traditions these are imaged as outside forces—such as seemingly impassable doorways or gates, demons, monsters, or the devil— and in other traditions as internal energies—ego, pride, narcissism, lust. In Jewish tradition we may call them *sitra d'atra/*the other side and *yetzer ha'ra*/the inclination toward ego-centered action (literally, "evil"). No matter what one calls them, or how one images them, barriers and distractions are part and parcel of every spiritual path. They may show up as an itch just when you are really getting into your meditation, a noise, an annoying person, random thoughts, sexual arousal—you name it.

Our immediate response is often to get rid of it, to push it away with our strength and will. But that is like those old slapstick comedies with the flypaper stuck on the bottom of somebody's shoe. Try to get rid of it and it just sticks to another part of the body. In that sense, what we resist is what we get. A healthier, more effective way of dealing with the problems will, at first, seem contrary to our intention. That is, invite them in. Welcome them. Make them part of your prayer. See them not as strangers out to get you but as your old friends who are just as much a part of you as your higher aspirations. After all, when all is said and done, most of the time they are inside your head.

When we invite the barriers to be part of our prayer, we can begin to transform them, to neutralize them or even turn them into something positive, to capitalize on the energy that they bring, misdirected though it may be. Striking this pose, we can laugh at them and at ourselves, taking away some of their power. "There you are again, you old rascal." These barriers and distractions, which seem so formidable when we are fighting them off, lose their scariness when we bring them into the house. And when the time comes, if any of them turn into real dragons, then we will gird ourselves to do battle.

In the meantime, the best thing we can try to accomplish is to give ourselves wholly and fully to our prayer. Letting go can be the most scary thing we could do. We begin by admitting that we have no ultimate control. This is like a spiritual trust fall. And then we place ourselves in God's hands. That is one of the images in the *Adon Olam* prayer; "Into Your hands, I place my spirit. I will not be afraid." This can become a kind of chant or visualization that you may want to try before you begin to meditate or pray. It will be a difficult one for you control freaks reading this book. But insisting on personal control is probably the greatest barrier to true prayer. Don't beat yourself up for having it. Simply acknowledge it, and bring it with you as you lay down into God's hands.

Meditation

I know I have mentioned the word "meditation" several times already, and some of you are probably saying to yourselves, "I thought meditation was an Eastern spirituality thing, not Jewish." Actually, Judaism, like all religious traditions, has a long-standing relationship with the spiritual practice known as meditation. In Hebrew, the word is *hitbod'dut* (pronounced *heet-bo-d'doot*), literally "to be alone in oneself." Like the word for prayer, it is one of those reflexive verbs—actions done within the self. While there are many types of meditation, using a variety of techniques, meditation can best be understood as "focused energy."

When I began meditating in the late sixties, I used a mantra given to me through Transcendental Meditation. At that point I had no idea that I could turn to Judaism for practically the same thing. It was just not talked about in Jewish circles at that period in time. I have meditated, guided by different gurus, using TM, raja yoga, and other disciplines ever since. I like to sit in the afternoon or the morning, not every day, but often. Twenty minutes or so is all it takes. It is a real energizer. But, more important, I have worked toward the goal of "making my life a meditation." That is to say, I attempt to bring the awareness, the consciousness, the connectedness without attachment, the focused energy that I have gained through sitting to everything I do.

Many people get hung up on the particular practice of meditation—mantras, yantras (visualizations), chanting, breathing, color imagery, positions or postures, walking, dancing or whirling. All of these are effective. No one praxis is better than any other; the choice depends on the personality and proclivity of the individual. Each discipline aims at the same thing—blocking left-brain rational thinking so as to allow the mind to quiet itself. In order to do that, we must focus our energy on a single thing. That's it. So simple it takes a lifetime to master. Not that we ever get perfect at it, because the distractions never go completely away. But we can get better at it, so that the benefits can accrue and be tangibly realized.

To begin, pick a practice that feels right. Experiment. Breath meditation, while difficult to master, takes no training to begin. All you have to do is breathe, slowly, deeply and completely, in through the nose and out through the mouth. As thoughts come up, let them go or invite them in. Just keep breathing. You can sit in a comfortable chair or on the floor. You can even lie down, but if you do, there is a danger that you will fall asleep. Though there is nothing wrong with a good nap, sleeping is not the same as meditating. If you want to try a mantra, choose a sound, a word, or a short phrase that can elevate you, point you in a direction. God names are good for this. So are words like *sh'ma* or *halleluyah*. Repeat them, silently or out loud, over and over again. When you realize that you have stopped or that your mind has wandered, say the mantra word again.

Closely related to mantra is the practice of chanting, in which one sings a phrase or a verse over and over again. The six words of the *sh'ma* prayer would be an example of such a phrase. It could even be chanted in English—"Hear O Israel, Adonai is our God, Adonai is One." When chanting, we allow the words to come from deep in our throats, so that there is a vibrational quality to our voices. An alternative to chanting is the *niggun,* a melody without words. While there are many such melodies that have been passed along, there is also at least one unique *niggun* in each and every one of us. It is the music of our internal spheres, the vibrational tone of our electromagnetic energy. In order to find your own *niggun,* all you have to do is listen for it (closing your eyes will help) and then allow it to come out. At first, you might hear other melodies, old songs that you have incorporated into your memory. But eventually (I have done this with hundreds of people in workshop settings) it will come out. And because it is your own, you will not forget it, though many people do like to record it just in case. Chanting a *niggun,* especially with eyes closed, is an excellent way to get ready for prayer, to slow yourself down during the day, to calm yourself in rush-hour traffic (though there it will probably be best if you keep your eyes open).

"I have been meditating for days and I haven't felt anything, Rabbi." At that point in the Zen story the Master smacks the person with a bamboo pole. Meditation is not a goal; it is a process, a technique, which, when used over a lifetime, will help the devotee with quieting the mind and staying focused. It is a powerful tool, easy to learn, difficult to master, for personal transformation, which can be used anytime and just about anywhere, even during "silent prayer" at your congregational worship services. And even if you never get "really good at it," the slowing down that it will cause you to do will actually benefit your physical health as well.

Prayerphernalia

There are three ritual objects that are used in Jewish worship to enhance prayer—the *tallit* or *tallis,* the *kippah* or *yarmulka,* and *t'fillin.*

The *tallit* is a prayer shawl. It can be made of any material and can be any color or size. On each of its four corners is a fringe, or *tzitzit,* which serves as a visual reminder of God's commandments. Most people wear a *tallit* only during prayer, but some Jews wear a smaller version as a kind of undergarment all day long.

I like to think of the *tallit* as the wings of the *Sheh-chee-nah,* the feminine immanent presence of God in our lives. When we wrap ourselves in the *tallit,* we are reminded that God is all around us, never very far away. I remember as a boy, standing next to my grandfather in synagogue and taking a corner of his *tallit* and draping it over my shoulder. In those moments I felt as if nothing could ever harm me. Today, whenever I am part of a congregation (instead of leading it from the *bimah*), I share my *tallit* with one of my children. Without saying a word, I feel like a link in a precious chain of tradition. My grandfather lives in my action and my memory.

The *tallit* has the practical effect of allowing us to be solitary in the midst of community. All we need to do is spread the *tallit* and put it over our heads. It blocks out everyone and everything, giving us private space for as long as we want or need it. And if you are not overly self-conscious, you can do this at any point in the worship service. Of course, this works best with a large *tallit,* not one of those skinny ones that we find at the entrance to the sanctuary. When I pray alone, my *tallit* usually stays spread out over my head the entire time.

A *kippah* is a skullcap. It is worn as an act of humility, to remind us there is something above us, greater than us. The *kippah,* too, can be made of any material, any color, any design. While some people wear one only when praying, others (like my oldest son) wear it all day long. The Hebrew root of *kippah* is the same as the word for the palm of the hand. I like to think of the *kippah* as God's hand on my head, stroking me in a type of loving parental gesture.

T'fillin, or phylacteries, are leather straps and boxes that contain scriptural verses that pertain to this ritual object. The Torah commands us to "bind these words on your hand and between your eyes." It does not tell us how to do that. *T'fillin* were created so that one could literally fulfill that commandment.

I think of the act of wrapping ourselves in *t'fillin* as a kind of betrothal ceremony. We are binding ourselves to God. Of course, that can be done without the physical object, but it is a powerful reminder and a visual symbol. In putting on the *t'fillin*, we quote the prophet Hosea, who saw his relationship to God as a kind of marriage, a covenant that, in this case, cannot be broken. The actual placement of the *t'fillin* touches those places in our body associated with the pathways to God—soul (the third eye in the center of the forehead), mind (the brain stem where the neck meets the shoulders), heart (the box on the arm lines up with our hearts), as well as the hands (symbol of everyday actions). The loop of the head *t'fillin* surrounds the spot in our skull that was once open and soft. Many spiritual systems understand this as the spot at which the soul enters and departs the body. In the Hindu system, these four are our highest *chakras*, or energy centers. The placement of the *t'fillin* is to remind us to seek God with the totality of our selves.

You may want to experiment with these prayerphernalia or create alternatives. They are intended to enhance prayer, to help you focus and get ready, not to be an encumbrance or to get in the way. Before investing in a *tallit*, you might want to try a blanket or shawl when praying and/or meditating. A rope or belt can give one the feeling of *t'fillin*. A hat or cap can substitute for a *kippah*. They may feel awkward or uncomfortable at first, so don't give up right away. Thirty days is a good trial period.

Choreography

What is the story with all this bowing and bending? Well, the bowing and bending of the knee all came about through our experience with monarchs. Bowing before the king, standing up when he entered the room, kneeling down as a sign of trust and respect—all these were once part and parcel of appropriate and decorous behavior. Inasmuch as we imaged God as King of Kings, all this "choreography" was transferred to the worship experience. The Hebrew root for knee is *beh-rehch,* the same root for the word *ba-rooch.* To bless God meant to "bend the knee."

The origin of movement in prayer, however, really stems from the words of the psalmist who implored us to praise God with every fiber of our being. How does one do that if prayer is a matter of the heart and the vocal cords? Through movement, sacred dance. In the ancient traditions, there were choirs, and orchestras, and dancers. Over the course of time some of these fell into disuse, made a comeback, disappeared again. Dancing was transformed into the movement of each individual worshiper. In the early Hasidic movement, many groups took the notion of praising God with every fiber to its maximum extent. Fervent worshipers could be seen doing somersaults while praying. *Shukling,* rhythmic swaying, became the norm. The mystical notion of prayer as "making love to the *Sheh-chee-nah*" was fulfilled through the gyrations, pelvic thrusts, and movement of the individual Hasid.

In the Sufi tradition, there are mystics whose "worship" consists entirely of spinning in circles. These "whirling dervishes" go into some kind of meditative trance through the spinning motion. I once watched one do it for hours; it was really amazing. It reminded me of what we used to do as kids. Getting dizzy was like getting high. None of us knew we were engaged in a rudimentary spiritual discipline.

With the coming of nineteenth-century rationalism, such notions were disparaged if not totally eschewed. Movement, especially during public worship, that was associated with sexual activity came to be seen as undignified. Soon, we were standing stiffly upright in prayer or sitting straight in the hard-backed pew, in which we could pay attention to the sermon. The 1950's, rock-and-roll music, and Elvis Presley began to challenge all that.

Today, with our focus on the whole person, movement in prayer—embodied spirituality—is once again a topic of discussion and exploration. Swaying, the movement of our arms and legs, can help us feel the prayers, not just say them. For those for whom the words have less power, the notion that they can pray with their bodies is incredibly liberating. Combining both, together with music, is a sense-filled and sensual experience. It brings us back to the moment in time when Miriam, timbrel in her hand, led the people in rejoicing their safe passage through the Sea of Reeds. Or when King David let forth an explosion of emotion by dancing at the dedication of the sacred Ark of the Covenant. My youngest son, Jesse, who cannot stand still when he hears music, intuitively understands all this. But, for those of us who grew up having to stand up straight and tall, movement can add an entirely new dimension to the prayer experience. If you are self-conscious about trying this in synagogue, you can try it out at home or when you are praying alone.

Blessing

Blessing is a kind of prayer that allows us to frame or shape a given experience. In Jewish tradition, we are challenged to say a hundred blessings every day. While many of those blessings would be included in the worship service, and since we are enjoined to pray three times a day one would get credit for lots of blessings just by attending services, still our day would be filled with little time-outs to think about God. We are engaged in all sorts of actions throughout our day—eating, commuting, exchanges with others, studying, creating, seeing elements of nature. We can simply have those experiences or we can attempt to raise them up, to turn them into holy moments of encounter, to move them from routine physical and mental acts to spiritual ones, to enrich ourselves and the action itself simply by bringing conscious awareness to what it is we are doing.

In our family, we say the *motzi* before we eat. We say it when we are at home or in a restaurant. Before we eat we pause, hold hands around the table, and say those ten words. It is not always easy to do. Sometimes we are in a hurry. Sometimes we do not feel like holding each other's hands. Sometimes it is a bit uncomfortable, especially during a fast-food stop on the road. But after years of beginning our meals this way, I can no more put a piece of food in my mouth or take a drink without thanking God for it than I could fly. Eating, a basic human animalistic behavior, has become a spiritual, religious act. We can fill our days with such moments through words of blessing. And yes, there is a blessing for everything—for seeing a rainbow, encountering a scholar, viewing a wonder of nature, doing a mitzvah, hearing thunder, meeting an elder, doing something for the very first time.

I know you are probably thinking that you do not know the words to all these blessings, and what are you going to do, carry a book around and stop to look them up each time? Well, if you were traveling in a foreign country, one in which you did not know the language, you would do that with a pocket dictionary. And you would use sign language, words you already memorized before the trip, even speak more slowly and loudly. But if you do not want to carry the "pocket blessing book," and you do not know the words of each blessing, just make up your own. You get the first six for free: *Bah-rooch Ah-tah Ah-doe-nigh, Eh-lo-hay-noo Meh-lech ha-o-lahm*/Beloved are You, Adonai our God, for _____." Just fill in the blank. We can say a blessing before and/or after the action. Either way, we transform both ourselves and the act itself. Our lives really are different when we add blessings to them.

And while we are on the topic of blessings, each of us can become a source of blessings for others who need them. In the ancient world, only the priest had the power to bless. After the destruction of the Holy Temple in Jerusalem, the rabbis passed that power, not to themselves as one might have expected but to each of us, you and I, everyone. A parent can bless his or her children. We do that every week at our Shabbat table—bless each of our children, by name, and kiss them to seal the words. We even bless them when they are traveling away from home, tell them to "feel it" around six o'clock that evening. Now that my parents spend the winter in Miami, my children insist that they bless me as well. Which they do. How can they say no to their grandchildren? And I love it. We can bless people who are in pain or who are suffering, be it physical, emotional, and/or spiritual. Bless their caretakers as well. To bless, to know that we are blessed, to be a blessing to others—this is a very powerful gift that we have the ability to bestow freely and openly. It costs nothing except a few moments of our time. But it means the world. And who knows? Perhaps, just perhaps, it will signal the beginning of our personal and planetary healing.

Discipline

When we think of prayer, the first word that comes to mind may not necessarily be "discipline," but, in fact, a fulfilling prayer life does require it. It is not enough just to pray whenever we feel like it. Like any great enterprise, this one too takes work and repetition. If I practiced the piano only when I felt like it, I might be able to play, depending on my talent and ability. But no one who has mastered the piano did so by playing only when the spirit moved him. He practiced so that he could be free to express himself and play.

Prayer is like that. While one can have a truly moving experience by attending a worship service once a year, the real rewards of praying and meditating come about only through hard work. That means we have to accept lots of so-so experiences, moments in which we "got nothing out of it." These moments are actually making possible the other moments of connection. They are our baseline, our database.

Praying when we don't feel like it often provides us with the breakthrough moments, or enables them to occur. It is in such moments as these when a word or a phrase may strike us in a new way—"So that's what that prayer is all about!" It is like driving down the same street every day and one day suddenly noticing a house or some other structure that clearly had to have been there all along but you simply never saw it. Moments like these snap us out of our complacency, help us to be more aware, remind us that there may very well be lots of other things "out there" that we are missing, simply because we did not see them, simply because we are not fully conscious. In that sense, our awareness is expanded. This is what the discipline of everyday prayer and blessing does for us.

Incorporating prayer into our schedules takes time. While there are those who will spend hours and hours on their prayer regimen—and if you have the room in your life, go for it—I believe we can accomplish the same or similar goals in a much shorter amount of time. In fact, I know we can. Some of us are even able to "multitask" prayer while doing other things, like exercising or driving in the car. It is the repetition that is the thing, not the number of reps. It is true with our bodies; it is true with our hearts and souls.

Devekut: *Clinging to God*

Once there was a king who wanted to test the devotion of his subjects. So he hid in his palace, announcing that he was there if they wanted to find him. At each doorway and in each nook and cranny, he placed optical illusions—gold, jewels, personal fame, monsters. One by one, the subjects were attracted to or frightened off by the illusions, so that they discontinued the search. In the end, only a few were loyal enough to find the king in the castle.

We are the subjects. God is the king. And the Holy One waits for us in the castle that is our world. *Devekut* (pronounced *d'vay-coot*, literally "clinging to") is the mystical understanding of how we must seek. Finding God has to be that important to us, has to be a primary desire, a need in our lives, at least as important as all the "illusions" that occupy so much of our time and our energy, so much of our lives. It is easy to become distracted. The illusions are so tempting. And there is nothing intrinsically wrong with most of them. But ultimately they are just illusions; they will not bring us the feeling of peace and true happiness that we so desire.

When we are young, most of our challenges involve some type of conquest of the outer world—acquiring degrees, establishing a career, being accepted by someone else, creating a home, partnering, birthing and raising children. As we reach midlife, most of us begin to turn our gaze inward, asking ourselves the big questions—What is the meaning of life, my life? What have I really accomplished? What legacy am I leaving to those who will come after me? These questions can panic us, turn the whole thing into the much-talked-about crisis, which, when we take a close look at it, is really shown to be an attempt to escape answering. Or they can simply become the source of our search, this new bend in the journey, enriching us, deepening us, helping us to put "new wine" into our aging vessels. Religion is about asking these questions and providing us with direction for how best to answer them for ourselves. Our prayer life can be enhanced by asking ourselves and God for help with the answers.

I am not sure why it is that God hides. I am not sure if that is what God does consciously, like the king in the parable, or if it is merely the description of life's reality. In the world in which we live, the material and physical world, a world in which our perceptive mechanisms point us outward, God is not so obvious. We have to step out of that world by going within in order to see clearly, to see truly. We have to see with our hearts. Prayer is one of the ways we do that. The path of the heart.

Getting Started

How you get started will depend largely on whether you will want to pray alone or in community, or both. If you want to pray alone, there is a whole host of questions you need to answer. Of course, some of these questions will be answered through your experience, and you can make changes as you go along, finding that some things work better than others. But I do urge some consistency. The nature of prayer is such that there is an ebb and flow to the efficacy of all these practices. If we give up on them too soon, we may miss the real gifts they offer to those who stick to them. Having someone to talk to who is on the same path or a rabbi/teacher can help you decide when to make changes and when to press on.

When will you pray? Mornings? When you first get up? In the middle of the day, as a time-out from work? In the evening or before going to bed? How often? Every day? Once a week? Where? Indoors or outdoors? Sitting in your favorite chair, on a pillow or rug on the floor, or standing? What will your prayer consist of? I suggest some type of fixed prayer(s)—*keva*—and some spontaneous offerings—*kavannah*. Will you use a *siddur*, or will you just say those prayers you have committed to memory? A good home prayer book is *On the Doorposts of Your House*, but you might prefer a pocket-size one, in which case you will be limited to a traditional text. If you are okay with the language, then fine. I always travel with my Birnbaum *siddur*, and mentally make the changes to egalitarian language when and if I look at the English. If you incorporate meditation into your prayer, which technique will you use? Will you chant? Use music? Sing? Play a tape? Will you move around or dance, stretch or exercise? How much, if any, prayerphernalia will you use? Remember, if you do not want to invest in these items immediately, there are simple alternatives, like a shawl or blanket instead of a *tallit*. Will you set a time limit or just allow yourself as much time as you need to feel that you have made a God connection?

These are the questions you will need to answer in order to pray on your own. I wish I could tell you that there are dozens of Jewish prayer/meditation tapes for you to employ, or some regular "pray at home" television programs that you could tune in to. Unfortunately, these resources are relatively unavailable in the Jewish world.* If you want to pray alone as a Jew, you are still in the realm of making it up for yourself. Decide on the regimen that feels best to you. That might include some internal stretching on your part. I generally advise a minimum three-month trial period for any praxis. That amount of time should give you enough experience to realize if something is having a positive effect on you. Again, talking it over with someone who has been there is always helpful. After three months, you may want to continue or make some adjustments. Of course, if anything you try feels negative or even harmful, stop it immediately. Either you are using a process that is not good for you or you are doing it incorrectly. In either case, stopping is indicated. You can always come back to it at another time.

If it is communal prayer you are seeking, then you will need to do some "*shul* shopping." Call the local synagogues, find out when their various services are, and start attending. Most synagogues have more than one format for worship. You may be attracted to one and not the other. Some have formal services in

*My own book, *The Busy Soul*, formats several ten-minute spiritual workouts for people to try on their own. A tape is also available from In The Spirit Music.

the main sanctuary, but informal services in the chapel or a meeting room. Becoming part of a community and fitting into their customs, worship style, music, and the like takes some time. It is like building any other relationship; it cannot happen all at once. People often feel uncomfortable at first. That is normal. If the discomfort is so great that you cannot even pray, or if you feel like a pariah, you are probably in the wrong place. But be wary of the feeling. It may be disquieting or off-putting just because you are not used to it or because you are having to bend your needs and tastes to that of the group. So much of feeling comfortable in prayer is simply what we got used to as children. Change in this realm can be very unsettling. Work that through. Bending your will to that of the group can be very beneficial, especially in the realm of prayer. If you are "home" you will begin to feel that way within a relatively short amount of time.

Depending on the community, there may be *havurah* groups independent of the synagogue. These, too, can be an opportunity to pray in a group setting. Or, you may want to start your own. While ten is the optimum number for a minyan, I have often had wonderful, prayerful experiences with fewer than ten. Of course, if you start your own group, you will need to make many of the same decisions as you did when you prayed alone. Only this time, they will be group decisions that may allow for some degree of independence and individual choice. One word of caution: There are groups that pose as legitimate Jewish alternatives that are really cultlike in the way they operate. When checking out a new group, try to determine what its overall affiliation is, by whom the rabbi was ordained, and things of that nature. If the answers are suspicious, so is the group. You can always call the local Federation to find out what you need to know.

The Path of the Head:

Study

In the daily prayer book, in what I call the "warm-up section" of morning blessings, a startling statement is made. After a list of positive actions for which there is no limit in this world, with the assurance of unlimited reward in the world to come, the text says that the study of Torah is equal to all of these actions combined. Given that the statement was made by a rabbi who spent much of his time poring over the meaning of the Torah, it is a remarkable declaration nonetheless. It points to a notion that I think is uniquely Jewish. And that is, while other religions have a tradition of intellectual study that is highly respected, only Judaism says that such study, in and of itself, is a religious or spiritual endeavor. In other words, while some traditions eschew the intellectual/rational as "unspiritual," demanding that we control, diminish, or even block out that part of ourselves in order to achieve oneness with God, Judaism declares that the left brain can be a certain path to the One.

The person drawn to this path is called the *chacham*/the wise one. Wisdom is more than knowledge, and different from intuition. It is the combination of both of these after a lifetime of study. It is an intellectual path, a rational pursuit, an end unto itself, which at the same time seeks to serve the living and pay homage to the past. So important is the role of the *chacham* that the Talmud excuses him from morning prayers with others if he is busily engaged in the pursuit of an idea. Of course, he will pray later, the text suggests. Jewish tradition, we can infer, recognizes study to be a kind of prayer, a longing for the One.

When I sit with a text, trying to unlock its meaning, I feel the presence of every student who ever attempted the same. And since every mystery is a reflection of the Ultimate Mystery, I also feel the presence of God. In candlelit rooms, impoverished ghettos and *shtetls,* secret caves, world-renowned academies of learning, the parlors of the wealthy—wherever we have traveled, no matter the circumstance, Jews have dedicated themselves to the study of our rich textual resources. It is a lifeline. A powerful connection to the past, present, and future. A path to God.

The Talmud indicates that study of sacred texts is a commandment, and of course, there is a blessing for that as well. *Blessed are You, Adonai our God, Ruler of the Universe, who makes us holy with commandments, commanding us to immerse ourselves in the words of Torah.* The Hebrew for "immerse" is *la-ah-soak*, and it is one of the few Hebrew words whose meaning is very close to its sound in English. We are commanded to soak up these holy words, to make them part of us, to absorb them into our lives, into our very being. As for all paths, some will be drawn to this one more than others will, but each of us is capable to some extent, each of us will be enriched by the words of Torah that we learn and study.

In the European Jewish world before the Holocaust, study groups abounded in the synagogues, and they were not just for intellectuals, but for the common working people as well. There were study groups for machinists, for fur workers, and for house painters. They did not spend their entire day in the pursuit of holy words, as did the *yeshivah* students, but there were ample opportunities for them to study with people from similar walks of life. Today, study groups are once again appearing all over, especially for women, who were once denied access to our sacred texts. With the addition of the Internet, there is literally no limit to the amount of studying one can accomplish. On top of that, departments of Jewish studies exist in hundreds of universities, with outreach efforts into their communities and beyond. Adult education classes offered through Jewish Community Centers and synagogues have become the norm once again and are certain to expand even more in the years ahead. The desire to know and to grow is being realized (for many) through the intellectual pursuit of Torah. Once again in the Jewish world this path to God is being traveled by numerous individuals who have come to understand that the education they received in religious school growing up was simply not enough to satisfy their need to live a life of depth and meaning.

"I know this guy who studies Torah with a vengeance, is always quoting rabbi this and rabbi that, and is such an s.o.b. What good is this teaching if it produces people like that?" I wish I could say I have never been asked this question. Even more, I wish I could say it never happens. But I know it is true. I have witnessed it myself. The ancient sages also saw it and debated whether or not such a person should study at all, for his study could cast aspersions on the text itself. If he had not studied, we could excuse his behavior as that of an ignoramus. But a student of Torah?

Each of us is imperfect, a cracked vessel. When liquid is poured into a cracked vessel some will leak out. If the crack is large enough, then all of it will be gone. Torah is that liquid— life-giving water for our parched and thirsty souls. But if the soul is mean-spirited, or neurotic, or unhappy, then the Torah poured into it will often be affected, even distorted. When illness is layered over with religious ideology, we can wind up with some very dangerous people. Yes, it could happen that the Torah "fixes" the individual, patches up the cracks, heals the wounds. That would be our hope. But often that is a process that takes a lifetime, with many slips and failures (leaks) along the way. Torah does not heal us all at once, and I am suspicious of anyone who says it does.

Lifelong Study

A few years ago I was invited to a conference on the subject of lifelong learning, sponsored by the United Nations. I learned that the average "shelf life" of a college education today is four to five years. That is to say, if one does not upgrade his or her knowledge in a given field within four to five years after receiving that degree or taking those classes, it will be rendered practically useless or obsolete. Yet somehow many of us grew up with the notion that once we graduated from our religious studies at the ripe old age of thirteen (bar/bat mitzvah) or sixteen (confirmation) we were done. We knew everything we needed to know about Judaism and the life of the spirit.

Actually, Judaism has always held that lifelong study is a necessary component of a Jewish life. "Why does the Talmud begin on page 'b'?" the rabbi exhorts his students. "To teach us there is no real beginning and no real end. The Talmud is like a sea. We simply need to jump in and start swimming." What is true of the Talmud is true of all Jewish learning. It is so vast that no one can ever master it all. But on the other hand, there are so many points of entry that it is relatively easy to get started and stay engaged. (And what is true of Jewish learning is true of learning in general. With the explosion of scholarship, printing and publication, and today's Internet, it is virtually impossible today to be a master of any field of endeavor. This explains why our specializations are getting narrower and narrower all the time.)

We need to make study a lifelong endeavor not only because of the content but also because we are always changing and growing. We see the words and hear the teachings through the prism of our lives. As we are never quite the same, our experiences in life constantly shaping us, changing us, redefining who and what we thought we were, so too does our study reflect those contours. A passage here, a story there, take on new meaning with our own passage of time. When I was younger, could I really appreciate the issues of aging parents and their children? I thought I understood, that I was empathic and sensitive to the issues, but there is nothing like living through it and having those same questions and issues mirrored back to me through my study of the ancient texts. As I have become a parent, and as my own parents age, I read the texts on these subjects with new eyes and listen with new ears. The texts are no longer simply words or ideas; they have become the substance of my life.

It is a kind of arrogance ever to think that "we know it all" on a given topic. The command to study each and every day mitigates against this kind of arrogance. It says we can never know it all, for every day a new challenge, a new question, an old question posed in a new way, a new insight awaits us. Such are the gifts for those who make continual study a part of their lives.

Torah versus torah

The Torah is the five books of Moses, handwritten by a scribe on pieces of parchment, sewn together, and rolled onto wooden rollers to form a scroll. It is kept in the ark on the eastern wall of every synagogue, and taken out amid great pomp and ceremony to be read on Mondays and Thursdays (ancient market days), as well as on the Sabbath and holy days. It contains the stories and the laws beginning with the creation of the universe and ending with Moses and the people of Israel ready to cross over the Jordan River into the Land of Promise.

When we say the blessing for study, on the other hand, we are really talking about all of Jewish learning, small "t" torah, not the Torah. What constitutes this "torah"? Well, in a sense, all of torah can be seen as a commentary and/or response to the Torah. The ancients understood the Torah to be the word of God. Some took that literally, and others knew it to be a metaphor. Nevertheless, it was important for them to know exactly what God had in mind. The Torah is not always that clear or complete. Often it speaks in a kind of telegraphic language. And so two forms of commentary or interpretation began.

One form asked the question, "What is it that God demands of us?" The Torah says, "Honor your mother and father," but does not tell us what actions would be deemed honoring. The Torah says, "Keep the Sabbath holy," but does not tell us how, or what it means to be holy, for that matter. Additionally, new situations would arise that had not been conceived of by the Torah—like living outside the Land of Canaan, or praying once there was no longer any animal sacrifice—literally thousands of situations. To answer this question, the ancients developed a legal commentary that eventually came to be called *halachah*/the way, but understood as Jewish law. It told the adherent the way to go in order to do God's will. It answered the "What?" question. This form of questioning eventually led to the formation of Mishna, Gemara, Talmud, Codes, and Responsa (which continues to this day) as a way of answering new questions of what to do.

But "What?" was not the only question asked. Others wanted to know "Why?" And so the meaning of the text was probed. This second form of interpretation is known as *aggadah*, literally, "story," as it often uses parables and stories to make its point. The *aggadah* is where we will find much of Judaism's philosophical and theological concepts. It is speculative and imaginative literature, with almost no boundaries for what is acceptable. And so, in order to understand a puzzling section, such as why Abraham was willing to sacrifice his only son, the writer might have the patriarch quoting psalms (written centuries later by King David and others) or speaking to a character that did not exist in the Torah story itself. The *aggadah* attempts to fill in the blanks of the story in order to help us understand it, not to suggest what might have "really happened." There is no dogma or creed in the *aggadah*. No required beliefs are presented. Differences of interpretation often stand side by side without a final decision on who is right or wrong. The genres that utilize *aggadic* interpretation are midrash, kabbalah, folk tales, commentary, short stories, and poetry. The last three are still being written today. While the early *halachic* material often used *aggadah* to make its point, and one will sometimes find prescriptive behavior suggested in the *aggadic*, the two genres are generally separate and distinct.

All of these interpretative texts together form "torah." And we see that even within this left brain spirituality, as I call it, there are some overlaps, two types of students. One is more didactic, argumentative, legalistic, the other is more literary, expansive, artistic. But I would take it a step further and say that "torah" is also teaching. Anytime one is studying any text or subject that enhances spiritual growth, I call that torah as well. History can be torah, art can be torah, learning to read Hebrew can certainly be torah, and if it helps you to discover who you are in your relationship to God, even this book can be torah.

Is the Torah true?

I cannot tell you how many times I have been asked that question. What most people mean by it is, "Did it really happen the way it is reported in the Torah? Did God really speak to Moses, and did all those miracles actually take place?" The part they do not say, but that is implied, is, "Because if it did not really happen, then why do we believe in it? Why should we do anything that it says? Why do we even bother reading it anymore?"

The answer to these questions will depend, in large measure, on the hermeneutical or interpretive lens with which one reads the text itself. There are those who say, "Yes, everything the Torah reports happened just the way it says. It is literally, every word and comma, the word of God. All contradictions are only apparent contradictions. All errors, inaccuracies, historical anomalies—all these can be explained." While I recognize the appeal of such a response, I am not one of those people. I do not believe every word of the Torah to be literally the word of God; nevertheless, I do believe the Torah to be true.

Its truth does not rest on historical accuracy or authorship. For who can say what "really" happened, anyway? Is not all history an interpretation of the events on the part of the historian? Torah's truth rests on that which it teaches us about ourselves, about God, about life, relationships, morality, values, virtue, commitment, about what it means to be a human being and a Jew. Torah is true because of the questions it asks us, not always the answers it provides. Better than any book I have ever read, the Torah asks all the right questions, the ultimate questions that we, who seek a life of meaning and purpose, need to ponder. The Torah is true because it acts as a mirror into which we must look in order to see who and what we really are, a psychological-spiritual mirror to the soul, to the self. It is a clear mirror, a perfect mirror, one that we cannot escape once we look. A mirror of ultimate truth. And all its stories and all its rules serve as an incredibly vibrant companion that challenges and guides us on the journey that we each make.

There are, of course, many other ways to read the Torah. Some do see it as a history book or an archaeological guide. Others read it as myth or fiction—stories and poetry, entertainment with a moral. The Torah can be read as a secret code, waiting to be unraveled. Today, computers are being used to find the hidden messages. In medieval times some kabbalists used a number system known as *gammatria* to unlock the Torah's secrets. Still others see the Torah as a book of law with some interesting anecdotes. The Torah can be read as a record of the Jewish people's ancient encounter with God—a kind of communal diary kept by Moses and/or others; or as a historical-romantic novel describing the tumultuous, on-again, off-again relationship between this jealous God and a wayward people as negotiated by Moses the marriage therapist. The sequel, the middle section of the Bible, continues in much the same vein, with a host of prophets taking on the role of Moses. The scientific reading of the text, also known as the "historical-critical method," attempts to discover the actual text by comparing the Torah to other, similar ancient Near Eastern fragments and manuscripts. It also delves heavily into the subject of authorship, revealing that the Torah could not have been written by a single author but was edited over hundreds of years by a variety of anonymous scribes. A sociologist might see the Torah as the Jewish people's collection of folkways and mores, told in story form and attributed to a God for the authority that that would lend to following the customs of the ancestors. And a political scientist might argue that the Torah is an instrument created by the ruling class (the *kohanim*/priests) to justify their authority and control over the people.

I am sure there are other ways to view it as well. Nor are these ways mutually exclusive; we may find some truth, some insight from several of these approaches. I know, I do. Each of us who lives under the influence of Western civilization is an inheritor of this text. If we are to make sense of it, each of us must become an interpreter. Just as we would ask a physician his or her approach to medicine, or a psychologist which therapeutic method he or she values most, I think it fair to ask the hermeneutical question of the one who teaches the text to us. What we come away with in this encounter will be shaped in large measure by the approach we bring to it in the first place. Then we can decide for ourselves whether or not the Torah is true.

The Search for Truth

One of the books I read early on in my adult spiritual journey was Hermann Hesse's *Siddhartha*. I was impressed by the young prince's unwillingness to be satisfied with the reality that was presented to him in the confines of the palace. He wanted to know more. He wanted to know what was really "out there," and the only way to find out was to journey beyond the boundaries of what had been presented to him as the world itself.

Though there may have been a kernel of history at work, Hesse used the metaphor of the palace with its surrounding walls and the world that lay beyond as the paradigm for the personal journey and the search. Siddhartha's challenge is our own challenge. For each of us, the confined palace is our map of reality, that which we have inherited or been taught as true. In order to affirm whether or not that is all there is, we must be willing to search for truth wherever it leads us and then make that journey into uncharted territory. Some, like Siddhartha, will actually have to leave their homes. They will wander into forests, climb mountains, sail oceans, trek into deserts. Others, like an Emily Dickinson, will discover it in the attic of the house where they were born. And others, because they cannot or will not do otherwise, will remain in their comfortable palace, never venturing forth, never discovering themselves or life's meaning. Most of us, I am sure, will wind up somewhere in between.

When I was deciding which seminary I would attend to pursue my rabbinical studies, the thing that attracted me to Hebrew Union College, beyond the first year spent in Jerusalem (I really wanted to return to Israel), was its commitment to truth. There were no preconceived notions of who I would have to be in order to be a rabbi. Rather, the journey into the world of rabbinic learning was opened up to me so that I could discover myself in the context of that world. I learned how to learn. And I learned that the search for truth, while it utilizes intellectual, rational faculties, is indeed a spiritual one, one that requires trust and faith. Anytime we are willing to open ourselves in that way, laying ourselves bare, placing all that we know for sure up for grabs, then we are in the realm of spirit. To this day, I attempt to read every book, listen to every lecture and every person, with the attitude that I know nothing, and am willing to go wherever the truth will lead me.

Rarely does a class go by in which someone does not eventually ask, "But what would an Orthodox rabbi say?" After I remind them that orthodoxy is not a monolith, and that there was and is a wide range of opinions within orthodoxy on almost any given subject, I give my standard response. There are basically two attitudes toward truth. The first says there is only one truth (and they happen to have it), and the other says there are multiple truths or many levels of truth. The first we call "orthodox" (literally "right doctrine") or fundamentalist; the second we call pluralist. I would argue that the spirit of Judaism is best reflected in the latter.

The Torah is not a math book. You cannot turn to the back and find the answers. It is a reflective text, like a prism. The more colors we see, the better. The rabbis always encouraged multiple understandings and multiple visions of the truth. That is why differing understandings were always printed on the same page, with no decision as to which was right and which was wrong. Even dissenting minority opinions were preserved. We have always argued over the truth. Today we believe this. Who knows what we will understand tomorrow?

There are so many visions of truth out there today, a veritable marketplace of ideas competing for your mind and your loyalty. How does one decide? I will agree that it is not easy. And jumping back and forth, while it may be beneficial for a while, will ultimately confuse the seeker and paralyze one's progress. If this is an intellectual path, then we must allow our intellect and common sense to decide. Which seems correct to you? That God would present one path for all of humanity to follow? Or that God gives us many paths, all leading to the same place?

Torah l'ishmah/*Studying for Its Own Sake*

As a product of Western education, I have always had a pragmatic view of learning—if I want to know something, I go out and read about it, study it until I feel satisfied by what I have learned. *Torah l'ishmah* (pronounced, leesh-mah) is the exact opposite. It posits that learning ought to be for its own sake, with no practical considerations or any ulterior motive. Though it is not the reason we engage in it, it is this type of learning that truly enables us to grow in spirit.

My own spiritual journey began in earnest when I began to study *l'ishmah*. Of course, I was involved in a variety of Eastern disciplines at the time, far from my Jewish origins. I practiced both hatha and then raja yoga, learned the principles of Transcendental Meditation, immersed myself in the teachings of Buddhism and Hinduism. It was the first time I was studying outside of a school system, pursuing no degree, with no direction certain, other than to know and to grow. As in most things I have done, I set out upon a rigorous course of study, creating reading lists and deadlines, keeping a journal of reflections, underlining in the books, taking notes. I was a serious student, but I was learning for the sake of learning. After I left the public school system, I taught at Denver Free University and other centers of the human potential movement. Ironically, I discovered *Torah l'ishmah* outside the Jewish world.

Later, as I began to integrate my Jewish self into my personal and spiritual growth, I approached it in the same way. My first "tool" was *The Pentateuch and Haftorahs*, edited by Rabbi J. H. Hertz, which I read religiously every Saturday morning. I continue that practice to this day, some twenty-five years later, though after three years I began to use several other commentaries in addition to Hertz. On Shabbat, it is my custom not to read anything that I need for work—no mail, no preparing for classes later in the week, no material for sermons, and no writing. I look at nothing practical, which is also ironic, because some of the most useful knowledge I have ever gained is that which I have gathered by studying for its own sake. Perhaps that is the spiritual message underlying this approach to "head spirituality." We can plan and we can plot and oftentimes we will eat the fruit of our endeavors. On the other hand, there is much to be gained from simply jumping in without a map or a compass. Both are rational and left brain. Both provide us with a path to God that is compelling, powerful, and very real.

This is the approach we take in our Torah groups at our synagogue. Using the ancient Palestinian triennial cycle (one third of the portion each week), we gather every Shabbat morning to study the Torah portion of the week. What began with a dozen people has grown now to more than one hundred, with latecomers sitting three-deep in the introductory group. There is also an advanced group in which the participants prepare during the week, seminar style, to present a particular approach to the text. A new group formed to study the Talmud. No degrees or certificates are awarded. We give no formal recognition to any of the students. There is no attendance taken, no official beginning, and certainly no end. I see my own teaching as a learning process; in fact, I have learned as much by teaching the text as I have by studying it. Both are a gift, the most precious gift of the spirit I have ever received.

Kabbalah

We hear so much about the mysteries of the Kabbalah these days, and the secret powers it bestows on its adherents—mind reading, inner peace, stock tips, forecasting the future, you name it. Actually, the word "kabbalah" means "received." It is a term used for the teachings of mysticism, which has had a long and important role in the history of Jewish learning and tradition. But it is often misunderstood and misappropriated. Mystics are not miracle workers. Nor are they charlatans looking to rip us off. They are serious seekers after God, whose primary goal in life is to become one with the One. Kabbalah is the body of literature that guides them in their quest.

There are actually two streams of kabbalah. One is made up of various practices, such as meditation, visualization, chanting, and breathing. This is called "practical kabbalah," but a more accurate term would be "praxis kabbalah," in that the knowledge to be acquired comes as a result of focused effort or praxis and is not necessarily practical in the way we usually understand that term. This stream fits more appropriately under the rubric of Heart Spirituality. The other stream is "textual kabbalah," which attempts to plumb the mind of God through various interpretations of the Torah. Remember the decoder rings when you were a child? You got some type of grid that enabled you to find secret messages embedded in a given text. The assumption of textual kabbalah is that the Torah is a secret code that can be unlocked only when we have the appropriate key. The most well known of these keys is the *sepherot*, or energy spheres of the *Zohar*. When it is properly applied to the Torah, which is taught only in the master-disciple relationship, we discover the inner workings of the mind of God, which provides the avenue par excellence for merger with the Holy One. In fact, kabbalah teaches that we are always a part of the One; it is merely our physicality and ego that trick us into believing otherwise.

Entrance into a kabbalistic circle was always carefully guarded and limited. The antinomian nature of the literature, its use of sexual and erotic imagery (what better metaphor is there for merger experiences?), and its heavy reliance on difficult philosophical constructs led to a rather narrow profile of those who would be allowed to study it—male, over forty years old, a "full belly of Torah" (i.e., learned and observant), and married with children. Warnings concerning those who tried to enter this form of study and lost their minds, their way, and even their lives were well known. And so it had a reputation as being elitist. Nevertheless, though it was never really extremely popular with the masses, and it was disdained by some leaders, mysticism almost always occupied a position of respect and awe in Jewish life. That is, until the Enlightenment.

With the advent of modernity, and the ascension of rationalism, mysticism began to be repressed in the Jewish world. Popular mystics like Jacob Frank and Shabbetai Tzvi turned out to be frauds, deluding their adherents and robbing them of their material possessions. The university eschewed anything that smacked of superstition or unprovable mystery. Jews flocked to the university and the world of science as ways of leaving ghettoization behind. Acceptance, harshly denied for nearly two millennia, was offered at the price of mysticism, ritual, and particularism. Jews were only too willing to pay the price. As a result, a rich tradition of kabbalah was repressed, nearly lost. In modernity, Professor Gershom Scholem of Hebrew University in Jerusalem rescued mysticism and made it an acceptable academic endeavor. Once again, that particular path was opened for those drawn to it. Today's popularization tends to trivialize the teachings, however, oversimplifying them for the sake of commercialism. Few teachers remain who can both reveal its mysteries and at the same time be open to the modern world and its appropriate demands of equality and intellectual honesty.

Hebrew

"When God gave Moses the Ten Commandments," five-year-old Samantha began in one of our Sunday morning prayer services, "did He speak Hebrew?" In the seconds it took me to formulate my response, I wondered if I should tell the children that the Hebrew alphabet was formed out of fire in heaven and that the letters came drifting down to earth, sent by God. These were magical letters, and the magic is still in them, but only if you love them and study them. "No one knows for sure, since only Moses would have heard it," I replied. "But this we do know. The only language the Jewish people have always used . . . we have used a lot of languages for speaking to one another, but only one have we always used, and that is Hebrew."

Hebrew is the sacred language of our people, the language of the Torah, and the primary language of every other sacred text. We do find some Aramaic in the Talmud and other sources, especially when they record conversations between sages who spoke it as their native tongue; similarly, we find great scholars borrowing key phrases and words in Old French, Arabic, Ladino, or Yiddish to explain important concepts to their students. Though one may pray or study in the vernacular, knowledge of Hebrew must be the goal of every would-be literate Jew. There is an authenticity that one can achieve only by first reading the Hebrew words and then actually understanding what they mean. Hebrew puts us closer to the tradition, and knowing the tradition brings us closer to God.

"It says Shabbat . . . it says Shabbat!" She was excitedly pointing to a challah plate in the gift shop window. We had just completed our adult *b'nai mitzvah* class session that day, and for the first time after months of learning to recognize the letters, Shari was able to make out a word on her own. In all my years of teaching, I know I have never seen anyone that excited about learning anything before. In that moment, the lines became letters and the letters became a word and she saw it, knew it, and called it out. Four thousand years rolled into a single word and it was magical, even holy. In medieval times, the rabbis would place a bit of honey on the alphabet books of the students in the hope that their study of Hebrew would always be sweet. I could imagine no sweeter moment than this one. It will remain etched in my memory forever.

Studying with Commentary

Martin Luther was the first Christian to publicly state that human beings did not need the Church in order to connect to God. One aspect of his "Reformation" was the principle of *sola scriptura*. Simply stated, *sola scriptura* implies that all one needs to do is read the Bible with an open heart and the Holy Spirit will enter that person, guiding him or her in the way of the Lord. However, nothing could be more antithetical to the Jewish way of reading or studying Torah.

When a Jew sits down to study a Torah portion, she or he is surrounded by centuries of scholars known as the *m'for-sheem*, literally, "the explainers or clarifiers." We never use only a Bible. We study with a text called a *chumash*, which consists of the text itself, sometimes with one or two translations (Onkelos's Aramaic and/or the spoken language of the student), the prophetic portions read in conjunction with the Torah known as the *Haftarah*, and, various commentaries. These commentaries often form the majority of the printed word on the page. Some versions of the *chumash* may have only one commentator; others will have several, each with his own point of view on the meaning and message of the text itself. No one commentator is authoritative. There is never just one way of understanding a Torah text. But some commentators have stood the test of time.

The most famous commentator was Rashi, Rabbi Shlomo ben

Yitzhaki, who lived in France at the end of the eleventh century. A successful vintner by profession, Rashi wrote commentaries on both the Bible and the Talmud. So essential is his understanding of the text, that for centuries no one would even think about studying the Torah or Talmud without his edifying commentary. And he did it all without a computer! Nachmanides (the Ramban) often disagreed with Rashi and would unabashedly say, "The Master has erred." Since he lived after Rashi, there was never an opportunity for the Master to reply.

Studying with commentary reminds us that we are never alone, that our endeavor to understand the text is part of a chain of tradition. It places us squarely in that tradition, helping us, stretching us to see points of view other than our own. When we read several commentaries we realize that all interpretation is multiple and various, reflecting the worldview and values of the one who is doing the interpreting. Texts are not stagnant. They do not mean the same thing to all people. That they contain pluralistic possibilities should not surprise us. Truth is like white light, which we know is composed of the many colors of the rainbow. Which color we see will depend more on us, the angle of our approach, the openness of our eyes. Seeing one color but recognizing that there are others needs to be part of our spiritual training, teaching us humility, patience, empathy, and acceptance. No one of us can ever get it all, all by ourselves. We are all part of a bigger picture, completing one another even as we work to complete ourselves.

Chavruto/*Studying with Others*

Just as we have the spiritual and intellectual presence of the commentators with us when we study, we are also told to have a *chaver*, (pronounced chah-vair; *chavruto* is pronounced chav-roo-toe) a partner with whom we work. Our partner needs to be at a level similar to our own, kind of like tennis. Too advanced, we get our butts kicked. Not advanced enough, we don't get much out of it. Jewish study is almost always communitarian. We study with others and, at the same time, the study itself helps to create community. When we share holy words, when we seek meaning, when we explore the recesses of our inner selves, when we argue over what is essential, which values matter most, what we ought to do and when we ought to be doing it, these conversations create the basis of community—a safe space for us to be challenged, accepted, and grow. I still have a special place in my heart for my study *chaver* from my first three years in rabbinic school. Though we do not see each other very often, or talk that much when we do, I know we both realize and continue to feel the bond that was created by our studying together.

What was said of the spiritual challenges of studying with commentaries can also be said of studying with others. With real-life, flesh-and-blood people, it may even be more of a challenge. Now I have to listen to others, even those I have already written off in my mind as irrelevant, talking to hear themselves speak, shallow, brownnosers, too traditional, not traditional enough— have I left anyone off your list? We all do it. Dismiss others with no real criteria for doing so. Studying with others forces us to listen, to open ourselves up to the truth of what the other is saying, to wait our turn, to weigh our words before we share them. After all, they may be thinking those same negative thoughts about us as we have of them.

Having a study partner or group also has the practical effect of keeping us on track. It is easy to make and break promises to ourselves. How many diets, exercise plans, and worthy goals have we begun and ended? The good intention is there, but it is too difficult for most of us to sustain on our own. Committing ourselves to a study group is a very powerful conductor. It makes us part of something larger than ourselves even as we wrestle with words and ideas that are also larger than we are. It becomes a good habit. And just like bad ones, they are hard to break.

Teachers

The Wisdom of the Sages known in Hebrew as *Pirke Avot*, urges us to acquire a teacher so that we can advance in our studies. While there is much we can do on our own, and while a study partner or group will definitely help us grow, ultimately we each need someone to call our teacher or *rebbe* if we are going to make true spiritual progress. And though it is possible to learn from many teachers and many different systems, there comes a point in each person's journey when he or she must trust one individual to guide him or her to the next step.

I have been fortunate to have had a few such teachers along my journey who have been able to be there for me. They did so without ego or pride, sharing their wisdom but allowing me to find my own, lovingly but firmly pushing me toward my highest truth, honesty, and integrity. A teacher does not try to make it easy for the pupil, and none of mine have erred in this regard. In fact, some of the toughest lessons I have ever had to learn were brought to me by my teachers. They were there for me in my struggle and my questions. They were there to pick me up when I stumbled, helping me to regain my own footing. They were role models, attempting to live the lives they talked about. They were open about their own failures and shared their stories freely. Though accepting, they did not shy away from judgment when it was necessary. Open to anything I would bring them, they helped me explore life's mysteries and God's secrets without being paralyzed by fear. They helped me discover myself.

Different teachers may help us with different tasks, and some may be there for us at a particular moment in time but not at others. Or we may find a single teacher who will be there for our entire life. Most teachers will be alive and vital, but there are times when we can rely on a teacher who is deceased. We learn from their words, as well as their personae, the stories of their lives. I have often looked to the work and life of Abraham Joshua Heschel to help me in moments of struggle and doubt. And the Bratzlaver Hasidim have never had a *rebbe* since the death of Reb Nachman. They use his stories as their guide. Over the years, I have from time to time written to authors of books I have read. The ones who respond are true teachers.

I know of no one who has ever made this spiritual journey without a teacher, but I have heard of many who lost their way without one. It is an act of faith and trust to call someone "teacher" and be willing to be led by his or her guidance. It is more than our lives that we entrust to them; it is our very being. While it may be difficult to find exactly the right teacher, it is essential that we try. In the process we may find some who are not perfect but who can help us or hold us nevertheless.

How Important Are Minutiae?

Unfortunately, the long history of Christian-Jewish relations has often been marked by rancor and harsh debate. One of the criticisms leveled at Judaism is its almost obsessive concerns with "hairsplitting arguments over legalisms," irrelevant conversations over nothing, matters that are hardly "religious." What constitutes a blemish on an animal to be sacrificed? How does one know exactly when to begin the morning prayer? How much milk would render a meat pot unusable? Is this really what religion is all about?

I hope you have seen, especially in this section on the Path of the Head, that nothing could be further from the Jewish perspective on this issue. For the *halachic* personality, the question is, and has always been, "What is it that God expects me to do?"

That, and nothing more. The *halachic* stream of interpretation seeks to do God's will exactly. There can be no approximate, no getting into the general vicinity, no best guesses. He wants to do God's will. Doing God's will is to be one with the Creator; the more exact, the closer the connection. And if it takes several pages of questions and answers so that he feels comfortable that he has gotten there, so be it. When it comes to serving the Lord, we want to do it right, the way God wants. Period. What might appear to be hairsplitting legalisms from the outside, is actually an intellectual-spiritual path to the One. Judaism has always accepted and encouraged this path, and while one might use his or her intellect in order to distance from God, we understand that it, too, can be a direct line.

Your Home Library

A colleague of mine once remarked, "I always know when I am in the home of someone who has chosen Judaism—there are so many Jewish books on the shelves." It is the mark of a Jewish home to be a place in which Jewish topics are studied and discussed. An essential part of such conversations are the Jewish books that one reads and keeps there.

Of course, every home should have a *Tanach*/Bible and a *chumash*/Torah with commentary. A home *siddur*/prayer book is also an essential. After that, it is really up to the person's personal interests and proclivities. Fortunately or not, there is no one authoritative list for such a home library; every rabbi will tell you his or her favorites. So that is what I decided to do as well. Here is my list of books I often recommend:

As a Driven Leaf, by Milton Steinberg—a beautiful novel on the search for self

The Last of the Just, by Andre Schwarz-Bart—a haunting novel on the meaning of Judaism

A History of the Jews, by Paul Johnson—best one-volume history available

God in Search of Man and *The Sabbath,* by Abraham Joshua Heschel—a compelling philosophy/theology of Judaism

A Guide to the Jewish Holidays, by Michael Strassfield—a practical guide to knowing and living the holy days

Settings of Silver, by Stephen Wylen—a very thoughtful basic Judaism book

The Ten Rungs, by Martin Buber—a good introduction to the world of Hasidic thought

Major Trends in Jewish Mysticism, by Gershom Scholem—a bit difficult, but honest and clear

The Source, by James Michener—still a great introduction to Israel; remember, it is a novel

Voices of Wisdom by Francine Klagsburn—accessible textual resources on a variety of subjects

Jewish Literacy by Joseph Telushkin—an easy-to-use "mini-encyclopedia"

The Thirteen Petalled Rose by Adin Steinsalz—a beautifully written book in the mystical tradition

Night, by Elie Wiesel—powerful witness to the Holocaust

Encyclopedia Judaica—a great place to begin on any Jewish topic

Three good magazines—*Tikkun, Moment,* and *The Jerusalem Report*

Getting Started

The good news is that there are so many opportunities for Jewish learning these days. The bad news is that with so many opportunities it can be a bit overwhelming and confusing. My best suggestion is to begin by picking a single subject or topic that interests you. It could be history, or philosophy, the Holocaust, Israel, the holidays—whatever calls to you. The Encyclopedia Judaica is always a good place to begin your initial research. At the end of every article, there will be a bibliography if you want to go further.

Another good way to begin, especially if you do not have a particular interest you want to pursue, is to read the Torah portion of the week with a good commentary. I recommend the one by Rabbi Gunther Plaut, *The Torah: A Modern Commentary*, published by the UAHC [Union of American Hebrew Congregations] Press. You will also need a Jewish calendar to look up the portion. Most banks have these calendars. It is a good way to begin, since the portions come in manageable sizes, readable on a weekly basis. I suggest Shabbat morning as a good time to do so. The other reason it is good to begin this way is that the Torah covers just about every imaginable Jewish topic. In reading through the Torah, one gets the best introduction to Judaism available. If there is a good Torah study group in your community, join it. While it may feel awkward at first, several months into it you will feel like a "regular."

Lots of people want to begin with an all-purpose, everything-you-ever-wanted-to-know-about-Judaism-in-a-single-volume source. Most of those books are fairly worthless. They either skip too much or generalize to the point of distortion. I could say the same about books that want to make Judaism "easy" or monochromatic. Judaism is not an easy religious path. It often includes many sides to a single question, valuing the dialectic that can exist between people and points of view. When an author or teacher says, "Judaism teaches . . ." and presents only one answer, watch out! Judaism is the religion par excellence that almost always has, "On one hand . . . but on the other hand . . ." Also, try to find out as much about the author/teacher as possible. While we are not limited to it, we are all products of our training. You should know if someone has had liberal or orthodox training. It will be an influence on what he or she says.

Almost every major Jewish bookstore has a Judaica section, these days. There are also Jewish bookstores in most major cities. Public libraries also carry books of Jewish interest. Of course, synagogues and Jewish Community Centers have libraries as well. In addition, there is a vast amount of material on-line, but remember to check out the source of the material. There are all kinds of groups "publishing" on-line, and it is not always easy to find out where they are coming from.

Adult education has really taken off in most communities nowadays. Call your local synagogue, Jewish Community Center, or university and ask for its current catalog of offerings. There are also long-distance opportunities to learn for continuing education or through Jewish centers like Spertus College in Chicago. Jewish Theological Seminary offers wonderful opportunities for interactive study on-line. Pick just one course that sounds interesting and try it. It may exhaust your need to find out about that subject, lead you to want to know more, or be a bust. Not to worry. We have all taken courses that failed to meet our expectations. There is always the next class. Taking a class will also present you with the possibility of meeting up with a rabbi/teacher who can guide you in your future studies. Many communities have study groups organized by synagogues, community centers, or individuals. The Jewish bookstore or local university will often have a bulletin board announcing these opportunities.

Most rabbis will be happy to meet with you and help you chart a course of study. If one is not available, check out All Experts on-line. Just ask a question, and a certified rabbi will

respond. You could even ask for me or write me directly at
<u>rebbeaid@aol.com</u>. It can be a bit overwhelming to begin—so
many books and so little time. I always tell potential converts
that it takes about seven years of dedicated pursuit to feel really
grounded in Jewish life and thought. Remember, Jewish knowledge is like an ocean. You will not be able to swim it all; no
one can. But you can jump in, get very wet, and be refreshed.

The Path of the Hands and Feet:

Action

In the blessing that Jews recite before beginning a meal, we say, "Blessed are You, Adonai, our God, Ruler of the Universe, who brings forth bread from the earth." The prayer thanks God for bringing bread out of the earth. When I was a little boy, I had visions of Wonder Breads, already in their distinctive plastic wrap, growing out of the ground, free for the picking. Obviously, the prayer cannot be taken literally. But Hebrew has a word for wheat as well as for every other grain. So why didn't the rabbis of old simply have us thank God for wheat? Instead, they chose to teach us a valuable lesson. We can thank God for bread because we, human beings, have turned that wheat into bread. We are God's partners, completing the act of creation by our own actions. God creates the potential, the intention; through our actions, we provide the completion. Through the use of our own hands and feet, we become God's hands and feet in this world.

The term for one who is God's partner is *hasid*/pious one. We usually think of piety as otherworldliness. In Judaism it is the one who is involved *in* the world. The name has become associated with the eighteenth-century radical movement later known as Hasidism. It was antiintellectual, appealing to poor, working Jews who could not afford to send their children to the academies of learning, the yeshivahs. Its founder, who was called the *Ba'al Shem Tov*/Master of the Good Name, was himself an uneducated man who appears to have been a tavern owner. He taught, with great spiritual insight, that if we would take on just a single mitzvah/commandment and make it our own, so that our lives became synonymous with that act, then it would be as if we had performed all the commandments combined. He suggested the following image: by performing this positive action, this mitzvah, it was as if we took hold of the hem of God's garment. When God felt that tug, the Holy One would reach down and pull us up the rest of the way. In other words, doing even a single commandment is a way of reaching toward and connecting to God.

Which commandment? Well, that depends on us, our individual natural tendencies, that which calls out to us. In the film *The Year of Living Dangerously* the photographer Billy (played by Linda Hunt) is asked why he doesn't try to get involved in the larger political issues facing his country, thereby helping more people. He responds, "I support the view that you just don't think about the major issues; you just do whatever you can about the misery that is in front of you, add your light to the sum of light." In Jewish terms, he is doing the mitzvah that has presented itself to him. We need not do more than that. In fact, that may be all that we are capable of accomplishing with our lives. But even if we did that and no more, our world would be a healthier, better place. Each day we are confronted with possibilities, opportunities to make a difference. Judaism calls on us to take on those opportunities one at a time.

Oftentimes, I meet people who say to me that they are not very religious. So I ask them to talk about their lives, and they tell me they are supporting several families from the former Soviet

Union who came to this country with virtually nothing, running a business in which the employees come first, taking care of their aging parents who just moved into their home, and half a dozen other things on behalf of others. Those are religious, spiritual acts as far as Judaism is concerned. That the individual does not deem them to be such usually means that he or she is not God-focused in performing these acts or does not connect them to the will of God. Such people are just doing what they believe to be the right thing. They also don't necessarily feel the presence of God when they are doing these acts on behalf of others. God is "not with them," looking over their shoulder, filling them with a sense of holiness. While I feel no need to disabuse them of their feelings, I do point out that religion is not just about praying to God, or thinking "religious" thoughts, or feeling spiritual. It includes simple actions that we can do each and every day.

While some religious systems may eschew the physical world as being base, or beneath the concern of God, Judaism has taught that our involvement in worldly matters can be a true path to the One. In fact, given the reality of our humanness, it is a path that none of us can totally avoid. The challenge is not to escape or ignore this world or ourselves; the challenge is to transform our actions into the service of God and others.

According to the mystic Rabbi Isaac Luria, in the beginning, there was nothing in creation but God. In order to create the world, then, God had to purposely contract in order to make room for the world to exist. This, however, created a space devoid of God's presence. Vessels were filled with God's light, to be placed throughout the creation, but then the cataclysm took place. The vessels could not contain the light and so they shattered, casting the shards and fragments of light everywhere. Thereafter, it became the goal of every human being to search out the pieces of vessels and redeem the sparks wherever they may be found. This act, he called *"tikkun olam,"* (pronounced tee-koon o-lahm) the repair of the world, restoring it to its true intention.

The world we live in is broken and in need of repair. It is filled with hunger and homelessness, poverty and pain. Inequalities exist between men and women, between the races, between nations. Discrimination continues, despite laws that try to protect us. Many labor for less than minimum wage; millions have no adequate health care. Disease and famine continue to ravage far too many nations. Dictatorships rob people of basic human rights. The inhumanity of war rages in spite of all our education and advanced learning that should have led us to peace. Violence and abuse terrorize our cities, destroy families, and cut short far too many young lives. All one needs to do is read the newspaper to recognize that there are still sparks of God's light waiting to be redeemed. Our world is not yet what God intended it to be.

Every action we take to repair the brokenness of our world, to make it a better place in which to live, frees another spark or lights it within another human being. Every time we volunteer at the soup kitchen, or work for justice legislation, or demonstrate on behalf of a righteous cause, or help make peace between individuals or nations, we are participating in the act of *tikkun olam*. At our synagogue's Mitzvah Day, on which some one thousand adults and children work on projects to improve our community, we begin with a blessing I wrote to help people be conscious of this fact, to help them realize they are doing God's work, not simply doing the right thing, when they labor on behalf of others. It begins with the same ten words that begin every blessing that speaks of commandment—*Bah-rooch Ah-tah Ah-doe-nigh Eh-lo-hay-noo meh-lech ha-o-lahm, ah-shehr keed-shah-noo b'meetz-voe-tahv v'tzee-vah-noo*—and then ends with the particular action about to be undertaken—*l'tah-ken eht ha-o-lahm*/Blessed are You, Adonai our God, Ruler of the Universe, who makes us holy with commandments, commanding us to take actions that help repair the world.

Though this may not have been the sense that Rabbi Isaac Luria intended in sixteenth-century Safed, in our own day, *tikkun olam*, largely through the efforts of the Reform Movement, has become identified with the prophetic call for justice generally translated as "social action." In fact, the Reform Movement maintains a Religious Action Center in both Washington, D.C., and Jerusalem in order to devote itself to this work. While not every person will be drawn to this particular path, I think it safe to say that every religious tradition imagines a world in which the needs of all human beings are provided and the brokenness that dominates our lives is repaired and healed. *Tikkun olam* helps to re-create the world the way it is supposed to be for all people everywhere.

In every community of which I have been a part, there seem to be some people whom you can always count on whenever a task needs to be done. My son Jonah is one of those people. No matter how odious or labor-intensive the job might be, if someone needs help, Jonah is there. Nothing is too difficult or demanding. Just give him a task and watch the work get done.

I am not sure what the quality is that creates such a person. But I do know that no community could exist without them. They labor without seeking any recompense or recognition. They are the first to volunteer and usually the last to go home. They sustain us and our world, blessing us in all our endeavors, as they, too, are a blessing in our lives. This chapter describes the various actions one can take to repair our world. It also challenges us to think about the actions we are already taking in new, spiritual ways.

G'milut Hasadim/*Acts of Love and Kindness*

Not all acts taken on behalf of others have social justice implications. There are myriad simple acts of love and kindness that we can perform as we go about our daily lives. Helping someone with a problem, saying please and thank you, smiling, showing hospitality, welcoming newcomers to our neighborhoods or our schools, visiting the sick, comforting the bereaved, being a "big brother or big sister" to a troubled child, helping a blind person to cross the street—is there any end to the goodness we can bring into the world simply by being loving and kind?

It is said in Jewish tradition that the Temple in Jerusalem was destroyed because of senseless hatred between brothers and sisters. What if we created a world in which there was "senseless love," a term suggested by Rabbi Shmya Shmotkin? Or, as the bumper sticker used to say, what if we performed random acts of kindness? Each of us has the capacity to do just that. It is just as easy to be nice as it is to be nasty, and it feels so much better. Only when we are feeling diminished, unlovable, do we act in ways that are hurtful to others. It is always a lack in ourselves that causes us to be cruel or unkind. But the emptiness we feel is never filled by hurtful words or actions. Quite the opposite happens; it usually adds to our loneliness.

My parents taught us, when we were children, never to go to bed angry at another person. To this day, I try to live up to that challenge. It makes for a better night's sleep. Similarly, whenever I receive a negative letter or complaint and my initial response is to answer back in anger, I wait a day or two to respond. Sometimes I share my return letter with a trusted ally. I've thrown out quite a few rough drafts. The second or third response usually says it better, without the rough edges.

There are so many people who make our lives better, easier. Though they are often "just doing their jobs," I like to thank them. I say it at the cemetery to the grave diggers or to the custodians at work. When my fabulous assistant, Claudia, leaves for home, I say, "Thank you for today." I try to learn everyone's name and use it when I greet them. I always compliment Karen on the dinner she prepares. And in a house with all boys, we always put the toilet seat down.

I have this thing about paying for tolls. If at all possible, I never use the correct-change lane. I feel that if there are still people working there, we owe it to them to drive through their lanes, and let them know that a machine is not the same as a person. I always greet them, ask them how they are doing, thank them, and wish them a good day. I do the same with the growing number of security gatekeepers here in Miami. It drives my wife crazy, but for me it is a recognition of our common humanity, a way of adding some love and kindness to our world. It takes an extra second, but I think it's worth it. Now if I can only do the same for all the drivers who make me crazy out there on the road!

Work

Most of us have to or will work at some point in our lives. In fact, most of us will spend a majority of our lives in the workplace, whether that be in or out of the home. We work for economic gain. But we also work to be productive, to make a difference in the world, to utilize our particular skills and talents, to stay busy and active, or simply because we would not know what to do with our time otherwise. Work is an important aspect of our self-esteem and gives us a sense that we matter somehow. That is why people often work way beyond their financial need to do so and why people who are unemployed often feel depressed, frustrated, or angry.

Ideally, work should be an expression of our mission in life. Each of us is here for a purpose, a reason. My mission is to bring people closer to themselves, to one another, and to God. Being a rabbi is the tool I have used for more than sixteen years to effect my reason for being. It is a good tool, but certainly not the only one. When I taught high school, I was basically doing the same work. Even when I did catering, or massage therapy, or managed an apartment building, my mission was the same. It is essential for each of us to discover our true mission. Since work occupies so much of our lives, it is of great benefit, both to ourselves and to the world, if our work helps us to achieve our mission. When it does not, or when it actually hinders that mission, we become diminished, unhappy, even angry, and empty inside. When people are unhappy with their work, it is often because that work does not allow them to fulfill their true mission in life. Simply making money will never substitute for personal mission.

Additionally, work affords us opportunities to demonstrate acts of love and kindness toward our coworkers and our clients, patients, or customers—the people we serve. I like to use the word "serve" when it comes to describing my own work. It reminds me of how I should approach my daily tasks. Perhaps it could work for you as well. In some occupations, work affords us opportunities to repair the world of its brokenness. And all work challenges us to be honest and behave ethically.

Remember the road sign MEN AT WORK? Today, some of those signs read, PEOPLE WORKING. When we work with the consciousness described here, we could post a sign reading, GOD AT WORK, for that is truly what happens when we transform our work into service and the fulfillment of a positive mission. Perhaps, then, instead of going to work begrudgingly, we can look at it in terms of, "how can I be of service today?" What can I do or say, in the course of simply doing my job, that will make my life and the lives of those around me happier, healthier, more complete?

Honesty and Ethics

In the *Shulchan Aruch*, the great Jewish law code of Joseph Karo, a full third of the collection deals with business transactions. It is a recognition that the world of work has the potential to place us in situations that test our values and morality. Why? Because work revolves around power and money, two primal forces that can drive people to acts of desperation. People kill for money and for power. That, in and of itself, verifies their volatility. If work can do that, then it means we need principles such as honesty and ethics by which it can be conducted and controlled. Subjecting ourselves to such controls is a religious act.

A good friend of mine, a very successful stockbroker, uses the law stated in the Torah, "Thou shall not put a stumbling block before the blind" (Leviticus 19:14), to guide him in his transactions with his clients. Who is blind? According to Larry, everyone that comes to him seeking financial advice. The vision of his clients is limited to that which he tells them. They trust him to invest their money and protect their future. He knows he could easily take advantage of them, making excuses for his failures or his wrongdoing, blaming "the market." In every profession, the practitioner is the one who sees. If we are not guided by a set of principles that go above and beyond our personal gain, then we are prone to all sorts of abuse and misdealings. Obviously, the law or fear of getting caught is not enough. The prisons are full of people who thought they could get away with it. By acting honestly and ethically in the marketplace, we are doing more than being good people; we are fulfilling God's commandments. Or as the old church expression has it, "If it ain't good on Monday, it weren't no good on Sunday!" The work environment is the place that particularly challenges us to live out our moral and ethical convictions.

Tzedakah/*Financial Contributions*

When it comes to helping others financially, Judaism does not recognize the act of charity. Charity, which comes from the Latin *charos*, means "an act of love." We feel love for the other, and so we choose to help him or her. In Judaism, the word is *tzedakah* (pronounced tz'dah-kah), which comes from the root *tzedek*, meaning "righteous action." In Jewish thinking, to help the poor or needy with financial assistance is an act of righteousness, having nothing to do with whether or not I love the person needing my help. In fact, from the point of view of the needy party, my feelings about helping him are totally irrelevant. He needs my help. The more, the better. Feeling good about it serves only me. Of course, it would be nice if I gave with a full and happy heart. But most important is that I give.

The famed medieval rabbi Moses Maimonides recognized eight levels of *tzedakah*. He understood anonymous giving to be at a higher level than recognized giving because it protected the feelings of the recipient, who did not have to be beholden to any individual. Maimonides taught that putting someone to work is actually the highest form of all, because then the person is no longer dependent on the gifts of others. All giving, then, is always from the perspective of the recipient—what it does for him or her—not the giver.

I often hear negative feelings about the amount and level of recognition given to generous philanthropists. The number of plaques and named rooms, buildings, columns, and archways is truly ridiculous sometimes. Have you ever been invited to the Cohen program in the Schwartz room of the Goldberg building at the Smith pavilion on the Stein campus to sit in the Levi chair and watch the Loewi stage? On the other hand, sometimes attaching one's name to a gift can inspire others to do the same. Even if it simply goads them or shames them into it, it is a good thing because someone is being helped. Though it may go against the human instinct of self-preservation and looking out for number one, to give *tzedakah* is to do the right thing. And anyone who gives away money without having to do so earns my respect. Given all the baggage associated with money, giving it away, for any reason, is a truly spiritual act.

I am constantly amazed by the generosity I see in the Jewish community. Jews have incorporated the commandment to give to the poor and needy as a touchstone of their Jewish identity probably more than any other religious act. It is the mark of most

Jewish homes to have a *tzedakah* box, which is filled and donated on a regular basis. Often, there is more than one. The Talmud dictates that even those supported by the community fund are commanded to give to someone less fortunate than themselves.

One of the problems associated with philanthropy today is that it is often reduced to check writing by the adults in the family. One of the ways we seek to combat this in our own home is that on Friday evenings, before lighting the Sabbath candles, we place all of our change in the boxes we keep—one for Israel and one for projects here, in our local community. Then, each Chanukah we take one day to make gifts rather than receive them. We count up the *tzedakah* monies, to which I add a stack of new bills from the bank, and we divide and make decisions based on the many appeals we receive during the year. From the time they could express themselves, our children have always been a part of this process. They can both share their feelings about the causes we seek to help and get a tangible feeling for the money we send because they see it placed in front of them. Another thing we do at least once a year is to shop for items—clothing and food— that we will give away. This, too, helps make the act of *tzedakah* more real for our children.

A variation on this theme are the many "sport-a-thons" for which people raise money by obtaining pledges from friends and family. These are especially popular among kids, who can therefore combine their athletic interest with helping those in need. I have seen the smiles on many children's faces when they hand over a check for thousands of dollars that they raised by riding their bikes, or roller-blading for a worthy cause. At our synagogue, every bar or bat mitzvah student must take on a mitzvah project of his or her own as part of the studies. Many kids choose some form of *tzedakah* as a way of expressing their gratitude for all that they have. Others volunteer time. And some do both. It is a very powerful experience when children give away their own money or time to help someone else. I have been moved on many occasions, seeing all that they can and do accomplish.

It is said that God looks after the poor, the orphan, the stranger, and the widow; that is, the powerless in any society. By giving of our financial holdings, we truly become God's partner in helping those who have no one but the Holy One to help them. Given human nature and the imperfections of our world, there may always be those who need our help. While gifts of *tzedakah* may not erase poverty or the evils of society, they certainly help ease the pain and suffering that exist in our world. Perhaps for now that is the best we can do.

Exercise and Diet

Though it may be directly attributed to the endorphins kicking in, many people do feel a spiritual rush when they work out or exercise. In fact, I know of several people who try to combine their physical and spiritual workouts by either praying or chanting while they exercise. I sometimes do that as well.

That there is a connection between the body and the spirit has long been recognized by various systems of yoga, Tai Chi, sufi dancing, and others. These practices consciously combine physical movement, breathing, and spiritual or meditative focus. Some of the early Hasidic movements also tried to combine prayer with movement. When people ask me about my own "choreography" of prayer, I half jokingly refer to it as "prayeroebics." I believe that dance or bodily movement is a form of prayer.

As a former long-distance runner I recognize that there is something truly spiritual about pushing one's body to its limits. That people feel this "high," this sense of transcendence while exercising is therefore not a surprise. When one speaks to athletes, they discuss their regimens in almost spiritual language. Discipline, focus, conscious eating, repetition—these are terms that could be heard in any ashram or monastery. Of course, the danger in body consciousness is that it has the potential to become a kind of narcissism, selfish, almost neurotic focus on "perfecting" one's body. We certainly see that all around us. But, if held in proper perspective, that of understanding the body to be God's gift to us, then staying healthy can be an act of religious devotion and gratitude. In that sense our bodies can be a temple, a temporary structure dedicated to serving God's higher purposes here on earth.

What is true of exercising is also true of diet. Food can be a hedonistic act of self-indulgence, or it can be a spiritual act, serving God, adding to one's health, while providing a sense of physical enjoyment and self-gratification. The Jewish discipline surrounding food is called kashrut (pronounced kahsh-root). It is a system of rules developed over hundreds of years designed to turn the act of eating into a carefully worked-out spiritual praxis for daily living. In fact, I would say, deciding how and what we eat is probably one of the most significant spiritual choices we can make.

Having experimented with all sorts of diets, I "became kosher" in my late twenties. It has literally changed my life. In addition to the Jewish dietary laws, I have maintained my commitment to healthy foods without chemical additives. While it is certainly permitted, though I believe discouraged (the original diet given to Adam and Eve was a vegetarian one) I eat red meat only occasionally. As in many things, the concept behind kashrut is to create a broad middle ground between hedonism (eat whatever you want) and asceticism (eat sparingly from a very narrow range of foods). Judaism recognizes the physical pleasure associated with eating and enjoins us to enjoy our food. It is one of those many pleasures permitted to us as human beings.

A word about getting started with kashrut. I always caution people to start slowly. You may begin by stopping the consumption of shellfish and pork, or mixing milk and meat at the same meal. Creating a kosher kitchen is not complicated, but does take some decision making and a bit of work. I definitely recommend enlisting the help of someone who has been there and done it. Since there are so many choices as to the degree of observance in this realm—label reading versus *heksher* (and, then, which one), the home versus eating out, two sets of dishes, Passover, methods of cleaning, methods of *kashering*—search out all the possibilities and find someone you can talk to about the pros and cons. Keeping kosher is a large continuum. Discovering just where you feel most comfortable on that continuum may take a bit of experimentation.

While there have been many attempts over the centuries to associate kashrut with health principles (i.e., no pork because of fear of trichinosis, and so on) I believe these laws were promulgated to teach us discipline when it comes to our eating. Certain foods are permitted, and others are forbidden. Certain combinations of food are permitted, and others are forbidden. Kashrut speaks of limitations placed on us by a Higher Authority. By accepting these limitations, we recognize that we do not have ultimate control. Additionally, the dietary laws turn every act of eating, every order from a menu, every acceptance of an invitation to another's home, into an act of conscious awareness of who we are and what our place is in the universe. When we add a blessing to begin and/or end that meal, we once again recognize that God is the provider and we the recipient. It transforms our eating from a physical, animalistic act into a holy, spiritual one, and our kitchens/dining rooms into holy, spiritual spaces. And since we are sure to do this almost every day, it is a way to make a God connection, to do something spiritual without much effort on our parts.

Language

As Rabbi Joseph Telushkin so correctly points out in his book by the same title, words can heal and words can hurt. We live in a culture that does not take words so seriously. We are prone to teach that "sticks and stones may break my bones, but words can never harm me." Yet how untrue we know that to be. More of us have been more hurt by words than by any act of physical violence.

The ancients understood the power of words, and so they urged us to speak little and do much and, when we do speak, to focus on ourselves and not others. Gossip (*lah-shone ha-rah* in Hebrew, literally "evil talk") of any sort was strictly forbidden, as it was understood to destroy human and community relations. The fact that we report something that is "true" makes it gossip. If it is untrue, then it is libel or slander. Both must be avoided. We live in a culture of gossip, however, in which listening to and talking about the foibles and failures of others has been raised to an international pastime. Tell-all books sell millions of copies before they are even published. Our desire to know the intimate details of the lives of others, especially those in the public eye, has become a sick obsession, ruining reputations and relationships. I am not sure if gossip can ever be overcome.

Once, when speaking about this problem in a class I was teaching, one of the participants queried, "But if we don't talk about others, what would there be to talk about?" I responded, "We would have to talk about ourselves. Imagine how that might elevate and deepen our relationships, if all we shared was our own thoughts, ideas, and feelings? And listened as others did the same." I believe everyone thought I was crazy.

To refrain from speaking about others is a mitzvah. Every time we resist the urge to share that which we know about others, we deepen the bonds of trust that exist between us, and we allow others to create their own relationships, free from our meddling interference. What a gift that could be.

Refraining from Evil

We tend to think that if we resist doing something, then we have not really "done anything." Just ask the person in recovery who gets through a day without taking a drink whether or not that is an accomplishment. The truth is, way more than half the commandments are "Thou shalt nots." In other words, Jewish tradition understands that the urge to do negative things, to take advantage of and harm others, in both big and small ways, is real, existing inside each and every one of us. In fact, if it were not real, there would be no need to create these rules. I would never have to say to my eldest, "Ari, stop annoying your brother," if Ari did not do that as part of his daily regimen in life. The human capacity to do evil, even in people who are basically good, is ever-present, as psychological experiments and history have taught us. To resist this urge is also a spiritual act. While it may not add to the goodness in the world, it diminishes the evil; on balance, then, goodness is enhanced. So the next time you want to share some juicy gossip but stop yourself because you realize the person really doesn't need to hear it, know that you have made the world a better place.

It takes a lot of goodness just to maintain the status quo. One act of violence or evil can undermine so much goodness. Sometimes it feels like all the good deeds we do are just fingers and toes in the dike, stopping the leaks from becoming a flood threatening to overcome and wipe us all out. Despite our best efforts, it seems we make no progress on making the world the better place it is supposed to be. But without each of those fingers and toes, the world would be even worse. Every time we resist the urge to hurt another human being, or an animal, or our planet, we have patched another hole. And that is good.

Environment

In addition to our care for the world's inhabitants, our concern needs to extend to the environment itself, the world that we have inherited and need to leave to the next generation. In Judaism we say that the world and all that is in it really belong to God. We are only temporary residents—renters, if you will. Environmental consciousness has been part of Jewish tradition since the time of the Torah. There, we are commanded not to waste anything, to allow land to rest, to be kind to animals, to plant trees, to refrain from cutting down fruit-bearing trees, even those of an enemy during the time of war. All of these laws were later expanded by the rabbis, who saw us as caretakers of the planet, borrowing the land from future generations.

Concern for our planet and the creatures who dwell there is one way of showing our devotion to God. After all, this is God's creation. When one entrusts us with something precious of theirs, it is our sacred responsibility to treat it with care and return it in as good or better shape than when we received it.

A story is told of an old man planting an olive tree in the land of Israel. When a Roman soldier happens upon him, he inquires, "Old man, why are you planting this sapling? Don't you know that you will be long dead before it bears any fruit?" The old man replies, "Yes, indeed, I know that. But just as my parents planted trees so that I may eat, so do I plant for the generations yet to come."

Every time we recycle, or work to preserve endangered species, or diminish pollution by riding our bicycles or carpooling to work, or any of the myriad other things we can do to make our environment cleaner and healthier, we are participating in a spiritual act that says the world is worth preserving and passing down. It is mine not to abuse but only to use respectfully and take care of. In responding to our world in this manner, we find our place in the great chain of life, making a contribution to all those who will come after us.

Bikur Cholim/*Visiting the Sick*

Though I mentioned this earlier, under the category of acts of loving-kindness, I think it worthwhile to explore this hands-and-feet activity as its own special category. Over the years, I have visited thousands of people in hospitals, senior centers, homes, and hospices. One of the common threads I have noted is that when people are not physically well, they often feel untouchable, unlovable, worthless. This is heightened, of course, when the illness lasts over a period of time or when one is dying. By visiting someone who is ill, you are saying "No" to their feelings of being marginalized and "Yes" to their humanity. Our presence itself brings comfort and peace of mind. By talking about what is going on "out there," we bring the world to the confines of their isolated room. By listening to what they have to say, or to their complaints, we let them know that they still matter.

I am always careful to make physical contact as well. Holding a hand, stroking a forehead, these are acts that tell the person you are visiting that they are not disgusting and ugly, that even in a hospital gown, unshaven or without makeup, their beauty shines through. Most diseases are not contagious, yet when we are ill we often worry about giving it to someone else. Touch breaks down that fear and lets others know they are cared for and loved.

I also always offer to pray on their behalf. Saying a prayer for healing, whether in their presence or not, allows afflicted persons to know that you are thinking about them and hoping for their wholeness and well-being. As I have been told many times by the patients I have visited, "It may not change things, but it cannot hurt."

Chevre Kadisha/*Burial Society*

It has been said that America is a death-denying society. With our emphasis on youth and vitality, the absence of older images in most advertising, our "warehousing" of the elderly in old age homes, and our total professionalization of providing care for the dying and the dead, it is as if our concern is only for those who can stay young and productive. In the face of this, Judaism teaches that the greatest mitzvah we can do on behalf of others is to help them die and prepare their bodies for the funeral. It is a purely altruistic act, one for which the recipient can never return the favor. This time-honored action, to this day, is carried out by the traditional burial societies known as the *chevre kadisha*, (pronounced, chehv-rah k'dee-shah) literally "friends of holiness."

What do they do? When someone is dying, members come by to help sit vigil with the family. They read psalms that help prepare the soul for its journey into the next world of being and consciousness. When the soul leaves the body, they prepare the corpse for burial, washing it, dressing it in simple shrouds, and staying by its side until the time of the funeral. The body, once the house of the soul, is not abandoned just because the life force is no longer within. It is accorded the same respect as it was when in the land of the living. Often, members of the *chevre kadisha* will help the family make any final funeral arrangements, attend the funeral service, and begin the process of burial. All these actions are elements of love and respect that do not cease just because physical life has ended.

Death is not a scary thing. In fact, it can be quite beautiful. I will never forget sitting with my (then) fiancée Karen, my future father-in-law, and his father as he lay dying of cancer. What dignity he displayed. What love and respect was he shown. We sat in the darkened room as he labored for breath, and then, he relaxed as his soul left his body and he passed from this world to the next. Through our tears, we said the *Sh'ma,* and felt his spirit palpably touch ours. It was a privilege to have been there; a blessing we all shared. Though I have since been with many families in this moment of loss, I have never forgotten it, and I know that none of us ever will.

Many communities today are rediscovering the power of creating their own *chevre kadisha*. While they do not replace the professional funeral director, they can be a source of comfort to a bereaved family, who can know that their loved one is literally in caring hands.

Messiah/Messianic Age

Most religious traditions the world over imagine and hope for a better world. In Judaism, this hope has almost always been focused on the coming of the *mashiach*/messiah or the messianic age, and is stated in the *Aleinu* prayer just before the close of every worship service. We also express this hope at the *havdallah* service with which we end Shabbat, and toward the end of the Passover seder when we open the door for Elijah the prophet, herald of the messiah. Though conceptualizations vary, and while there is no one accepted creed or dogma in this regard, basically Judaism has divided itself into two major streams of thought on this subject. One says that the messianic time will begin whenever God deems it the right moment. In such a scheme, nothing we do as humans has any effect on God's decision.

But another, equally compelling, conceptualization teaches that when we act in such a way that indicates to God we are ready for the messianic age, then God will send this messenger to us. In other words, it is through our actions, the goodness we bring into the world, that the staging ground for the world's perfection and completion will be created. Though this will not occur in human time (which is, by its very nature, imperfect), it is a certain event that will usher in a new age of peace and equality for all. Therefore, anyone who works for the betterment of our world and the people in it brings us one step closer to the time of the messiah. Such is the power of every human act. Such is the power vested in each and every one of us.

The world we live in is still waiting to be redeemed. We could take the approach that one person doing his or her best will not change anything. After all, the problems are so vast, so overwhelming, is it not more than a little naïve to think we can make a difference? But who can really say which of the actions we take will be the one that saves us, that finally brings the hoped-for redemption? And even if it does not, think of the goodness we can add just by doing it.

Getting Started

In one of the workshops I do, I give people a blank calendar and ask them to fill in their typical week. As we begin to analyze their daily activities, I have them write down the letter 0 next to any action taken on behalf of another. You might want to try this yourself. Each 0 represents a spiritual act. Anytime we do something in which another person benefits, we are doing God's will, becoming an agent of the divine purpose. Every time we work to make the world a better place in which to live, we are being truly "religious" people. My sense is that there are many religious people in this world that do not go by that label. No matter. Perhaps in some ways it is even better that they do not. They are God's silent partners completing the work of creation each and every day.

There are so many opportunities to make the world a better place in which to live that it can be a bit overwhelming at times. In my own life, I receive from ten to twenty requests a month for my help, either financial or volunteer time, or both. I could literally make a full-time occupation of responding to each and every one of these requests—all of them from good causes that really need me. How does one decide what to do and what to ignore?

First, you must realize that you will say "no" to some very worthwhile endeavors and some very wonderful people. Our "no" is not a rejection of the cause or the person; it is merely a reflection of the reality of our limits. We need to know what we can legitimately accomplish, and how much time and resources we have available. When asked to volunteer for something, I always ask what all the expectations for that volunteer are. How many meetings and/or events per month? When do they take place? Any subcommittees? Any financial obligations? What skills or talents do they seek from their volunteers? I consider my volunteer commitments as serious as my professional ones. I never say "yes" unless I feel I can make a positive contribution.

Next, I try to match my own personal interests with the mission of the group that is calling upon me for support. There are many worthy causes that hold no interest for me personally. I usually do not get involved with those causes. I also turn down speaking engagements if the topic or format does not interest me. Again, that is not an expression against the topic, it is just a result of my abilities and interests. When one matches a personal interest with a cause, the likelihood that serious effort will be expended and positive success achieved is definitely increased. It will also help to ensure that you will stick to the task.

While one does not need a synagogue, a Federation of Jewish Philanthropies, or a Jewish Community Center to volunteer time, those institutions often do have connections with agencies that may meet your interests. Going through a larger institution may also put you in contact with others like yourself who have similar interests. The relationship between the synagogue and the other group is an ongoing one, thereby increasing the sense of commitment. On the practical side, you can spend more time on task and less time tracking down the group and setting up your volunteer experience. Most synagogues have social action committees with ongoing projects that might be of interest. Many of these committees are open to new members taking on new projects. So many worthwhile things in this world have been accomplished because one person got it started. Nowhere is that evidenced more than in a synagogue's social action committee. Lots of synagogues have what is called a "Mitzvah Day," on which volunteers go out on a number of worthy projects that have been created and organized by the committee. It is a great way to "get your feet wet," do some good, and feel great about yourself.

Most everyone I know is concerned about time. Modernity was supposed to free us up with all its modern conveniences, yet we are always rushing and never seem to have enough time. But it does not have to take forever to do good. We can volunteer on our lunch hour by going to a nearby school and tutoring a child who needs help. Or read to someone or help someone with a household chore. At work, we can show up with flowers. Or be a "secret buddy" by doing a good deed that goes unrecognized but makes someone's day that much brighter. How about smiling? While at the grocery, we could be shopping for that homebound person in our building, or for the soup kitchen. Making lunch? How about making another one for the homeless guy you pass on the way to work? Do you really need that doggie bag? I bet that homeless woman does. None of these acts takes extra time, but each of them makes a difference. I'm sure you can think of even more.

As the rabbis taught us, we do not have to finish the work all by ourselves. But we are not free to ignore our parts in this sacred task.

The Path of the Soul:

Relationships

The rabbis said that God dwells in the presence of love. No wonder. Our reaching out to another, overcoming our loneliness and isolation, brings the Divine Presence into our midst. We know that, we sense it, we have all felt it in our lives. The moment when all separation melted, and there was no me, no you, no it—when all was one. That is the presence of God.

I was once hiking with friends through some fields in the hills of Galilee in northern Israel. We came across a huge banana orchard. I don't know if you have ever seen bananas growing. I hadn't. What we call a banana is really part of the pistil and stamen structure of the flower that grows on the tree. As we looked at these miraculous creations, time seemed to stand still. We all felt it. Afterward, we tried to talk about it, what we felt, what we knew. It was as if we had become one with those trees, and one with each other. Thereafter, whenever we met, there was this knowing look that we shared. We had been in the presence of transcendence. And it was very real. Maybe the most real anything had ever been for any one of us. The philosopher Martin

Buber called it the I-Thou moment. A moment in which we are not experiencing the other; rather, we are in relation. A moment of true connection that can take place between people, things, the natural world, God. All of it was present for each of us that day.

Every relationship is a spiritual act. Anytime we extend ourselves, go beyond ourselves, act without concern for ourselves or our own self-preservation, it is a spiritual act. Any act that is nonrational, for which there is no logical explanation, that we perform out of love or conscience, is a spiritual act. Spiritual acts awaken us to what is special and holy in life. They give us a sense of connection to one another and to life itself, reminding us that we are not alone in this world. They help us to see that a great deal is at stake in our choices, and in the words we say to one another, and in the actions we perform, both large and small. They give us a taste of the infinite. Far from being an impediment, our relationships with one another and the world itself become a vehicle by which we recognize the sacredness of all life. Judaism teaches that our relationships with one another do not take place in a vacuum, they are not merely a private matter; rather, they are also the concern of God.

A full half of the 613 commandments of Jewish tradition deal with the actions we take in our relationships with one another (some of which were discussed in the chapter on hands and feet). Relationships provide us with myriad opportunities to do religious acts on behalf of other human beings—providing for their physical needs, visiting them when they are sick, comforting them when they are bereaved, teaching our children, honoring parents, speaking with care and concern, showing respect—the list could go on and on. They are known as *mitzvot bayn ah-dahm l'chah-vay-roe*/between one person and another. The things we do for one another are one of the primary ways we bring God into our lives and our world.

God has a stake in every relationship because God has a stake in our being whole. Only in relationship can we be fully human.

Only in relationship can we be truly whole. Relationships challenge our humanness. They call on us to accept without understanding, to contract ourselves in order to make room for the other, to join together physically and emotionally and yet to sense our separateness and our boundaries. Relationships encourage us to balance holding on with letting go, to make commitments and bind our lives by them, to be humble and admit our mistakes, to forgive and ask for forgiveness. We deny ourselves and delay gratification, we wait, we trust, accept limits, make sacrifices, and live by our deeds and not just by our words. All these make relationships possible. All these are part and parcel of the religious life. The one makes possible the other.

We have more relationship technology today than ever before. The bookstores have shelves filled with every manner of self-help to cure every relationship ill—how to be better lovers, better friends, better communicators. And in spite of all that, we find relationships in more trouble than ever before, and we are lonely. In the end we are human beings, noble, trying our best, but essentially flawed and imperfect. We meet one another not in some idealized fantasy where everything is perfect but in real life with all its agonies and joys. It is just these moments, these encounters in the world of the everyday, that offer us the possibility of opening our souls and coming to a fuller, richer awareness of what it means to be in relationship with one another. To experience the transcendence that we can bring into all our lives. This chapter points the way to that transcendence, in our relationships with others, in our relationship with ourselves, in our relationships with the world around us, and in our understanding of all of them.

B'tzelem Elohim/*In the Image of God*

The last ritual we perform in the *havdallah* service to conclude Shabbat, is the lifting of our fingers to the light of the braided candle. When we do that, we see the light of the candle sparkling in our fingernails. This light is to remind us of the primordial light of creation, the light God creates before the sun and the moon and the stars, the light of God that is in every human being. It is somewhat easier to see that light on the Sabbath when we have taken a full day to "re-soul" ourselves; to do it at *havdallah* reminds us to take that consciousness into the week ahead. Each of us, even that annoying guy at work, has a spark of the divine within.

The words *b'tzelem Elohim* (pronounced b'tzeh-lehm Eh-lo-heem) literally mean "in the image of God." Judaism teaches that each of us is created in the divine image. The myth of our creation story is voiced in the singular, Adam and Eve, not because primitive man thought we all proceeded from the same two human beings. They had eyes. They realized there were different races, characteristics, and the like. The story insists on one man and one woman in order to teach us a lesson about the meaning of creation. "Therefore the human being was created on its own to teach you that whoever destroys even one soul is regarded by the Torah as if s/he had destroyed an entire world; and whoever saves a soul, is regarded as if s/he had saved an entire world" (Mishna Sanhedrin). We are, each of us, an entire world. Unique. No one just like us ever existed before and no one ever will.

In contrast to some other religious traditions that would have us efface our personhood because it is seen as a barrier between ourselves and the Divine, Judaism insists that only so long as we are a person can we preserve our relationship with God. Each of us is equally significant before the One who created us as unique individuals, yet all in exactly the same way. And if it is true of our relationship with God, then it is true of our relationship with others. We need to see each person, not through the lens of their personality, or occupation, or the things they can do, or the limitations they have, but as *b'tzelem Elohim*, a minirepresentation of God in the universe. We need not lose ourselves in order to become one with the Divine. Ought it not be the same in our relationships with one another? And isn't that what we all ultimately want? To be loved and accepted just for who and what we are?

I remember, a number of years ago, I was introduced to a young woman who was a teacher. After a while, she asked me if I wanted to see a picture of the most beautiful child in the world, one of her students. "Sure. Why not?" came my reply. I was totally unprepared for the enlarged photograph she took out of an envelope. The child had Down's syndrome. He was smiling, a broad smile, obviously very happy. "Isn't he gorgeous?" she enthusiastically asked. Though I am ashamed to admit it, I could not see what she saw. I was too caught up with my own notions of beauty, and this boy did not fit my limited understanding. All I saw was a "retarded kid." She saw the spark of the Divine in this child, and that made him (and all of us) truly beautiful.

The Golden Rule

"Love your neighbor as yourself, I am Adonai." Most people believe that what has come to be known as the "Golden Rule" was first thought of by Jesus of Nazareth. Actually, he was simply quoting Leviticus 19:19. There, in the most extensive list of behaviors governing human relations that we find in the Bible, we discover this simple yet profound idea. God wants us to treat one another as we would like to be treated.

Imagine if we did just that. Before we said anything to another person, before we took an action that would affect their lives, we thought to ourselves, "How would this feel if it were directed at me?" And then we refrained from anything that had the potential to be hurtful or wounding. Wow!

But the Torah takes it one step further. This is not just about refraining from hurtful actions and words. It is about proactively behaving in a loving fashion; loving others as we, ourselves, would like to be loved. Love becomes the basis for human interaction. Love that is nurturing, that enables us to reach our full human potential, the kind of love we all need and want.

Do Not Covet

The exact opposite of loving your neighbor is coveting that which is his. And while we generally have to work at being more loving, coveting comes naturally and easily. Why do we covet? I guess part of it has to do with the proverbial grass looking greener over there on our neighbor's lawn. Another part probably has something to do with our own unhappiness or sense of incompleteness. We think to ourselves, "If only I had _____, then I would be content." But nothing that comes from outside the self can ever make us whole, can ever bring us the true happiness we seek. "Outside happiness" is like a drug: it will always be temporary, always wear off. And it is never as good the second and third time around. It cannot be. Only that which comes from within can remain with us.

To covet is to dehumanize the other. When we covet, we turn the other into an object or the sum total of his or her objects. We want the house or the car, the job or the power, the spouse, but we fail to recognize that all these "things" come with an entire series of attachments, relationships, and baggage. If we saw our neighbor as a complete human being, we would see all of this as well. But our coveting blinds us to the totality. And any thought or act that distorts reality can never be healthy, which is why it is forbidden. Coveting is insidious. It undermines the very fabric of our interpersonal relationships.

Patience

People close to me know that I hate waiting in line. Whenever there is a buffet meal, I am either first or last. It just seems such a waste of time to be waiting.

Recently, I was at the airport and I had to check in. No avoiding the line in that situation. As I watched this reservation agent checking each ticket and seat assignment, I thought to myself, "Can't this guy work any faster? Or is he purposely going slow to annoy me?!" And then I realized he was working as fast as he could. That was who he was. It had nothing to do with me.

Patience is about acceptance. Acceptance of others for who and what they are. Acceptance of a given situation over which we have little or no control. It is about getting ourselves out of the picture and realizing the world does not revolve around us. Patience points us to our humanity and our humility, if only we would listen, pay attention. I just may try waiting in that buffet line yet.

The Exercise of Power

In that same chapter 19 in the Book of Leviticus, we come across the most curious commandment: "Thou shalt not curse the deaf, nor put a stumbling block in front of the blind." While it would obviously be cruel to try to trip up a blind person, what difference would it possibly make if we cursed a deaf person? He cannot hear us anyway.

But this verse, along with others that instruct us in the treatment of strangers, orphans, and widows, are really lessons on the exercise of power, especially in the realm of relationships. When the Torah warns us against cursing the deaf, it does so precisely because we can do that, thinking all the while that we do so with impunity. But the truth is, by doing so we undermine the equality that ought to exist in our human interactions. Who would know? God would. And so would we. Though we could probably get away with it, it is precisely because we can that we are cautioned to be extra careful.

The rabbis extended these prohibitions to any situation in which we have a "one-up" power advantage. Such situations call on us to find the resources to act more God-like, taking extra precautions not to abuse the opportunity presented to us. It is not just the warning that God will take up the other person's case; rather, it is our understanding of what is being called forth from us in such situations.

Each of us is blind and/or deaf to something or other. There are numerous people in our lives whom we trust in areas of endeavor in which we have little or no knowledge. And there are others who place their trust in us, expecting us to do our best on their behalf. Yet it may happen, from time to time, that in spite of our best intentions, others around us do fall because of something we said or did. Sometimes they fall of their own accord. At such times, we do well to help them to their feet again, set them on their path, and do our best to keep it clear. And we can hope that they or others will be around for us when we stumble as well.

Derech Eretz/*Appropriate Living*

I still hold doors open for women. I do it for men as well. On buses and trains, I give up my seat for someone older than me. My parents called it common courtesy; the Jewish tradition calls it *derech eretz,* (pronounced deh-rehch eh-rehtz) literally "the way of the earth." Once upon a time, we took these behaviors for granted. Not everyone did them, but those who did not were considered rude or improperly raised. Today, in our postegalitarian society in which manners are considered chauvinistic if not downright imperialistic, it has become anything goes.

I would not argue for a return to the way things were. I hold no nostalgia for the past. But as I sit at the Yield sign, watching the fifteenth car in a row creep past me without the driver so much as glancing my way, I do wonder if we have lost a bit of the human touch. For that is what underlies the Jewish notion of *derech eretz*—the full humanity of the other. And since everyone else is no less human than I am, I "owe" them the same simple courtesies that I want to be afforded in public. Words like "excuse me," "please," "thank you," "I am sorry," "bless you" (when someone sneezes), "hi," "enjoy your day," and the like tend to humanize the public sphere. They are a recognition of the humanity of each and every person and are apt to increase the amount of decency we see in the world.

How we speak to one another is also part of this. There was a time when certain language was deemed inappropriate in public. It was not that we did not know those words; rather, we reserved them for certain settings and particular relationships. In our questioning of all our inherited values, this particular one seems to have gone out the window. We are now free to pronounce any vulgarity wherever and whenever we please. But when I stand on line at the movies with my nine-year-old to go see the only G- or PG-rated film at the multiplex theater, I wish he did not have to hear that women are "bitches" from some teenager and that every boss is a "f—ing ball breaker." Perhaps we need to have PG lines as well.

Boundaries

Every relationship is aided by clear boundaries, though they may, at first, feel like limitations. We have to know what the rules are, what is appropriate or acceptable, what is allowed, and what violates our sense of self, or propriety. We wear many hats, different ones with different people. Each relationship is also different. What is perfectly normal for one to do with a partner can be abnormal if done with one's child. Yet boundaries are violated all the time, creating wounds and scars that may take a lifetime to heal.

While I want to be friendly with my sons, letting them know they can always come to me for any need, I do not want to be their friend. Friends are people they will choose. Friends are equals. Friends will come and go throughout their lifetime. But (so far) they have only one father. They call me *abba,* Hebrew for "Daddy." I want to be their *abba,* and that means we have to have clear boundaries that spell out what our relationship is and what it is not. It is not always easy. But it has to be done. In part, all of us define ourselves through the relationships we create. If these relationships are distorted through boundary violations, then we will come away with a distorted sense of who we are, continuing the process in all or most of our relationships with others. Differing expectations can destroy the fabric of what the relationship ought to be about.

While sexual violations command the majority of our attention, there are many other sorts of violations that are just as insidious and can also be damaging or hurtful. In fact, I see victims of boundary violations all the time. Some are pernicious, downright evil. Others are more innocent, the result of childhood play or exploration. Many others are the by-products of unhealthy, even neurotic adults who simply did not realize what it was they were doing. Parents who share secrets about their spouse with their children; siblings who touch one another inappropriately; lack of privacy in the home; role confusion; enmeshed family relations that consider individual behavior to be acts of treason to the family unit; "favored children" or even teachers who have class favorites; sexual innuendo in both language and behavior; some types of flirting; and unwelcome touching are just some of the boundary violations that get passed off as normative behavior. But they are not.

Appropriate boundaries are really about seeing the person as she or he truly is; violations turn that person into someone or something else. Boundary violations are dehumanizing. At best, they create confusion. At worst, they create secret wounds that last a lifetime. In fact, that is what victims often hear—"Let's keep this our secret," "Don't tell anyone!" "If you tell, I will kill you!" Most individuals who were the victims of boundary violations as children will themselves violate boundaries as adults, unless they receive the appropriate therapy to help them finally "uncover it, talk openly about it, and break the cycle."

In the Torah, once the people have escaped Egypt and affirmed their covenant with God at Mount Sinai, they begin the work of hearing and receiving the law. Laws, rules, are boundaries. In their immaturity, in their inability to commit to One God, the people violate the rules again and again. The 1960's in this country were about liberation. Much good came from our examination of gender assumptions and cultural limitations. Civil rights, equal opportunity, desegregation, the women's movement were all positive outcomes. But to the extent that liberation calls for the throwing off of all limits, it can become very unhealthy, leading to the violation of the very limits that were meant to protect and keep us safe.

Responsibility

When my youngest was a toddler and something would happen around him, his immediate response was always "It's none of my fault!" It took us years to teach him that one can be responsible without being at fault. "Fault" carries a negative, accusatory connotation. "Responsible," on the other hand, is really more neutral. To be responsible simply means "to be (a) cause in the matter." Taking responsibility is a form of "showing up," being counted. It is a spiritual act, saying to God and others, "Here I am. What do you need?"

I do a fair amount of short-term couple counseling, mostly crisis intervention and premarital readiness. In fact, I insist that everyone who wants me to officiate at their wedding take a premarital survey and discuss the results with me. I also work with parents when they are having problems with child-rearing issues or sibling conflicts, and with adult children who are caring for aging parents. The number one problem I have is getting everyone to stop blaming each other for the situation and take responsibility for whatever led to seeking my help in the first place. Like my son Jesse when he was a toddler, many adults still feel that responsibility equals fault, and they do not want to wind up being the bad guy. I try to teach them what my mother taught me so long ago: "It takes two to tango." Every relationship, every aspect of every relationship, including the problems and conflicts, was created by at least two people. Unless and until we each take responsibility for what is happening to us, we will not have the ability to work on it, fix it, or let it go. How can we give something away if we do not own it in the first place?

So the next time you find yourself in a conflictual situation, begin by asking yourself, "How am I contributing to this conflict? What am I doing, saying, or not saying? What body language signs am I giving off that are adding to this problem?" You can then acknowledge those. I find that just doing that much helps diffuse many potential blow-ups. Of course, it is helpful if your partner does the same. After all, he or she is equally responsible.

Responsibility begins, then, with the willingness to look at the possibility that I was a cause in the matter. Simple. But so very difficult for us to do. It is much easier to blame someone else, especially if he or she is acting out. Today, when we are discovering more and more chemical or hormonal imbalances that are at the root of numerous psychological issues like depression, attention-deficit disorder, schizophrenia, and the like, we are more apt to blame the "disease" for the associated behavioral problems. Nevertheless, our responses and our reactions are our own. Whatever is happening in our lives, we are a contributing factor. Owning just that much, accepting it as true in and of itself, can strengthen our relationships and heal them of numerous wounds.

Forgiveness and Reconciliation

"For sins against God, the Day of Atonement atones. But for sins against another, the Day of Atonement does not atone, until one seeks and asks for forgiveness from the one whom he offended." I read that every year on Yom Kippur. It is an accurate summary of the Jewish theology of forgiveness. God's forgiveness is immediate and automatic. All we have to do is ask. But God can forgive us only for what we have done to violate our relationship with the One. God cannot forgive us for what we have done to another. For that, we have to go to the very person whom we have hurt. And he or she is required to forgive.

In the course of a day, a week, a year, given human limitation and imperfection, we and others will "sin." Sins are violations of the covenant, both written and verbal, that we have with God and with others. A sin can be seen as taking a step away from God or another; mitzvah, is taking a step toward God or another. All of our lives we are engaged in a dance, forward and back. While we all will do our best to avoid sinning in the first place, the real issue becomes what we do once we realize that we have sinned. Judaism is a very humanistic system in that it recognizes and accepts the reality of human sinning and provides a method of forgiveness and reconciliation that is quite accessible and psychologically sound. Not to do so would be tantamount to condemning one to carry those sins for a lifetime, a burden that would soon overwhelm even the strongest among us.

Once we recognize that we have sinned, and have accepted responsibility for it, our next step is to go to the offended party to apologize and ask for forgiveness. (This is called *t'shuvah*, (pronounced t'shoo-vah) which means "return"; we want, in essence, for the relationship to return to the way it was at the moment just before the sin.) Of course, our apology has to be sincere and contain within it the intention never to repeat the sin. This can only be an intention. Future behavior will determine whether or not our *t'shuvah* was complete. If we repeat the sin (and each of us repeats some sins with regularity—our life issues) then we know we still have work to do. The one who listens to our apology and our plea for forgiveness is expected to accept it and forgive us. Just as God does. Only then can reconciliation begin and the relationship be restored.

But what happens if those to whom we apologize do not accept it? Or refuse to listen to us? We have to try again. Perhaps they were not ready to let go. Perhaps their wound is too deep and not fully healed. Perhaps we appeared insincere. Perhaps they have been there before with us on this very same issue. Perhaps they will never be able to totally forgive us. Some sins are that great. Our task, though, is to apologize and seek their forgiveness. After all, it is we who sinned against them. Their task is to find the place in their soul to forgive. If they do not, then they will carry the burden. Just like the hot potato game we played as children. Once we have handed it off, it no longer is ours.

Of course, if we seek reconciliation, then forgiveness must be granted. It takes both parties to re-create any sense of relationship. But there can be forgiveness and a parting of the ways. Healing can take place even without reconciliation. For sins against God, Judaism teaches us that the Holy One automatically forgives us if we are sincere in our apology. That does not mean we "get off" without punishment. We can be forgiven and still be punished.

Punishment is the way we "pay for our sin," make restitution. Forgiveness is about putting the relationship back in order. If we are to be God-like, then we, too, must forgive.

I am often called in to mediate family disputes. The sins committed were real and have grown larger with the passage of time. Usually, both parties see themselves as the offended one. And both probably were. Sex and/or money are most often the root causes. The toughest ones involve sexual abuse. It is very difficult for the abused child to forgive the abuser. The abuser has difficulty taking full responsibility for the abuse. But if the apology is genuine, and the plea for forgiveness sincere, then the only one who is hurt by not accepting it is the one who has already been wounded by the sin. Kind of like a double whammy. It sounds unfair, I know, but it is true. Forgiving is our way of accepting any responsibility we may have had in the situation and letting go of the pain and the hurt.

Reconciliation becomes the work of reestablishing a relationship or creating it anew. This is hard work, especially if any baggage remains. Only a complete *t'shuvah* and genuine forgiveness can provide the ground for this work to begin.

Falling in Love

Who can say why two people meet and fall in love? It is without a doubt one of the beautiful mysteries of the universe, and it portends a truly wonderful moment in time for the two lovers. "Falling in love," writes M. Scott Peck in *The Road Less Traveled*, "is a temporary escape from the loneliness of our individual ego boundaries to a feeling of merger with our beloved, and with all of life." The sudden release of oneself from the isolation of self is experienced by most of us as ecstatic. We and our beloved are one. All things are possible, and nothing else matters. Time stands still and we are eternally present for our lover. The strength of our love will enable us to overcome any obstacle. We are lonely no more.

This experience of falling in love parallels the mystic's quest for merger with God, with all of life itself, the yearning for oneness that pervades the entire cosmos. In fact, the two are very similar. Both are highlighted by a temporary loss of boundary and the elimination of any sense of separation. Everything in this world hungers for unity. God is the ultimate unity. When we fall in love, love without ulterior motive, when the boundaries of the self disappear—no me, no you, no it—for that moment we achieve a oneness with the other, the world, and everything around us. No wonder couples who have fallen in love describe themselves as being "so much alike." And when couples come to me to talk about the possibility of divorce, they describe themselves as "so different." I wonder what happens to change them so radically in their years of being together.

Actually, they don't change that much. It is just that the "anesthesia" (a term, I believe, coined by Harville Hendricks) of the falling-in-love stage has finally worn off. Sooner or later, in response to the reality of daily living, individual identity will reassert itself. She wants to save money; he "needs" that Jaguar. She wants to go to Temple; he wants to watch the ball game on television. She really doesn't like his friends; to tell you the truth, he doesn't like hers either. Once again they are two separate individuals. They have fallen out of love, or so they think. And so they desperately seek "a new love that will never end" all over again.

We cannot maintain the merger state indefinitely. No one can. As important as this stage is for the formation of our romantic relationships, it cannot last forever. The honeymoon has to end so that the real work of staying in love can begin. There is no problem with falling in love. The problem for us today is that so many equate it with, mistake it for "being in love." And when the former ends—and end it must—they honestly believe something is wrong, that the love is over. As much as we ought to cherish our falling-in-love moments, we have to understand that love is made real by actions, and that is work.

One of the great misunderstandings many people have about Judaism is the notion of the "chosen people." Far from being a chauvinistic ego trip, the idea of chosenness simply indicates that for some mysterious reason (not because we were bigger, smarter, more powerful, better-looking than anyone else), God fell in love with Abram and Sarai (who would later become Abraham and Sarah), choosing them to form a people with whom God would create a marriage contract called the covenant. The terms of this covenant are spelled out in the Torah, which serves as a kind of *ketubah*. When we are reminded of this act of love in our daily liturgy, our response is to list those behaviors by which we demonstrate our love of God. Falling in love leads to the creation of relationship; staying in love is actualized by our actions. True love is more than a feeling. Love is an action, a welcome and endless task, something we do for one another. We fall out of love when we stop acting in love. In the long run it is the behaviors that drive the emotion, not vice versa. Do them, and the love will remain strong and vibrant.

Commitment

I remember one of the first weddings for which I was officiating, I asked the couple in a premarriage counseling session why they thought their marriage would beat the odds and last. They responded that they really wanted to stay married but that if it did not work out they could always get a divorce. I pointed out that while divorce has always been an acceptable, unstigmatized option in Judaism, our tradition points out that "even the altar of God sheds tears" when a marriage ends. With divorce so commonplace today, I am not sure they even heard me. They had not even started, and they already had the escape clause planned out. Just before the wedding, I lifted the bride's veil and asked the groom, "Is this the one you want to marry?" When he answered, "Yes," I asked her if she felt the same way. Commitment is our willingness to answer "yes" every day, our desire to make it work with this person, and not someone else.

We live in a disposable, I-want-it-yesterday kind of world. It seems that everything is either drive-through or delivered to us. My son told me the other day that my computer was slow because we had to wait about a minute and a half for it to download information from who knows where in cyberspace, information that in my days as a student would have taken me hours in the library, if I had even been able to charm the librarian into helping me. At a preschool Shabbat, I suggested to a parent that she allow her child to hold the little *kiddush* cup of grape juice while we chanted the blessing to help her child learn to delay her gratification. She looked at me like I was some type of alien.

Every relationship, good ones as well as bad ones, will "hit the wall," run into dead ends, seem like it can go no further. "And the people of Israel were encamped by the sea when Pharaoh and his warriors overtook them. . . . The people cried to Moses, 'Let us be and we will serve the Egyptians for it is better to serve them than die in this wilderness.' " Our initial reaction to such roadblocks is often to leave; our pain is great, our needs are not being met, we are frightened by an uncertain future. The past seems so much better, so much brighter. Staying requires an act of faith, of placing the relationship above the self and one's immediate needs or gratification. It is a test of our faith, our character, and our souls. (Of course, not every relationship is meant to continue. When there is real abuse, the best thing to do is get out and head for safety.)

When I was growing up, ballplayers stayed on one team their entire careers, companies did not move overseas for cheaper labor, and people stuck together in good times as well as bad times.

While not every relationship can or even should last forever—and Judaism has always allowed for divorce based on incompatibility—commitment is our willingness to hang in there. Without such commitment, the probability of a lasting relationship is rather dim. Just as God is committed to us in a covenant called the *brit,* so do we need to commit to our relationships in order to give them a chance to succeed. It has not always been smooth between us and God. There have been plenty of fights, accusations, and mutual disappointments. We have relied on counselors and therapists called prophets and rabbis. But here we are, after some three thousand years, still hanging in there with one another. Commitment. No relationship can hope to survive without it.

Trust

Without trust, there will be no commitment. No way. Trust comprises equal parts of experience and faith. Experience shows us that the people with whom we have entered into committed relationships are worthy of our trust. They are reliable, they do what they say they will do, they show up on time in all the appointed places, they refrain from actions and words they know will hurt us, they attempt to say and do those things that help us to feel safe and loved.

But experience is not enough. Trust also requires an act of faith. We have to believe in the other, especially when they fail or disappoint us. Of course, such faith has limits; it cannot be blind. It has to survive some reality checks. But without faith, no commitment can ever be complete. When Abram and Sarai say "yes" to the covenant with God and agree to leave their home and everything familiar, their trust is primarily based on faith. Later, they will have experiences that teach them that their trust in God was well placed. Their ten trials (as they are called) will let God know they were the right choice as well—even though they fail at some of them. In our relationships, too, sometimes faith comes before experience. But both are necessary for commitment to stay strong.

Trust is strengthened by clearly agreed-upon boundaries within which both partners live. The failure of the open marriage experiments merely reinforces this awareness. We need to know where our partners are. When they disappear on us, keeping too many secrets, trust is undermined. Of course we need private lives and independence. But these, too, must be in a context of clear boundaries. Otherwise, the ground of trust will be shaken and the commitment upon which it stands will almost always topple.

Acceptance (of Differences)

When a couple comes to me to talk about their desire to get married, somewhere in that first conversation I invariably ask, "Why? Why do you want to get married?" and they most always answer, "We love each other." "Of course you do," I respond, "Otherwise you would not be here in the first place. Now, why do you want to get married?" I am not looking for material for my wedding charge, though it helps. What I want to begin is a conversation on love, what it is and what it isn't, how it will grow and change, and the role it can play in their relationship.

Love requires an ability to adapt, an understanding of and acceptance of both self and others. When I meet the couple, they have already fallen in love. Everything is fairly harmonious. They are one. Once marriage sets in—and it does not matter how long they were together before the wedding day—they will begin to find out just how different they truly are. Will we be able to see our lover as whole in spite of those differences? When we begin to discover the inevitable limitations and imperfections, will we be able to see our partners as whole, just the way they are? Or will that part of me that thinks we ought to be the same (i.e., like me, because after all, my way is better) begin to resent him or her for being different?

The Torah teaches us that after Jacob was injured by the angel so that he walked with a limp for the rest of his life, he came "whole before God." In spite of his physical limitation, God saw him as whole. Can we see our loved ones as whole when they disappoint us? When they are not what we hoped they would be? When, in spite of our best efforts, we cannot change them, mold them, "perfect" them? When they don't say or do the right thing? When they are overweight and out of shape? When they lose their job or lose their way? When an expected and hoped-for baby cannot be conceived or is miscarried? When they are lying in the home for the aged and cannot even remember who we are? When they are sick or dying? When they fail to live up to their potential or their promises? When they break faith with the relationship itself? Every true relationship has its shadow underside—thoughts of separation, loss of faith and hope in the other, unexpected changes in our partner's values and behavior. Can we accept these without diminishing the wholeness of our partner? And what of the inevitable anger, frustration, resentment, loneliness, and despair that sometime or another rear themselves in a life lived with others? Can we accept these losses and limitations without blaming them on the ones we love?

No two people will ever be exactly alike. Even identical twins are not identical. If falling in love is about the blurring of differences, and getting divorced is the result of irreconcilable differences, then the work of relationship is about the successful negotiation of these inevitable differences—accepting them and/or seeing them as balance or strengths. Of course, such acceptance must be forthcoming from both partners. Mature love celebrates differences. Such a love can only be built on the acceptance of our partner's imperfections, faults, and differences—the things we do not particularly like. Such acceptance is never easy. It may come with maturity or by the recognition that we, too, want and need to be accepted by those we love. Just as God accepts us no matter how broken we are, no matter how many sins we commit, so we must learn to accept one another for who and what we are, not for what we would like them to be. Ultimately, every relationship is about how we negotiate differences.

Support

According to Lurianic kabbalah, in the beginning, God filled all time and space. So when God made the world, God had to retract in order to make some space for the world to exist. This voluntary contraction is called *tzimtzum* (pronounced tzeem-tzoom). And so it is with relationships. We have to give the other some space to become the person God meant him or her to be. As the contemporary teacher David Aaron says, "Only people who are full and have a strong sense of self can give space to another without the fear that they themselves will become empty." We have to be there for one another in the way others need us to be, not the way we think they ought to need us. And this is work we have to do by ourselves.

Another way of saying this is that being in love is having a stake in the growth and well-being of our partner. This does not mean that we are responsible for our partner's happiness. No one makes us happy. And no one ought to be blamed for our unhappiness. But we all need others to support our getting there. When we see a happy, healthy couple I guarantee that is exactly what they are doing for one another—each of them is supporting the other on their personal journey toward wholeness. Perhaps more than anything else, relationships are defined by how well we can do this for one another.

One of the places I have had to learn to do this in my own marriage is with Karen's circle of women friends and spiritual co-travelers. Karen has always had a rich group of women with whom she has explored her own spirituality. It was one of the main reasons she had difficulty in leaving our former home in Wisconsin. But within a couple of years here in Florida, she had done it again. While I ostensibly supported her activities in this regard, the truth is I was jealous and fearful. I noticed that every time she came home from being with the women, we would argue and snipe at each other. It wasn't until I confronted my own lack of friendship that I really got a handle on my feelings and began to truly encourage and enjoy her relationships that have nothing to do with me but everything to do with her own growth and happiness.

Altruism/Loss of Autonomy

True love, whether it is the love of spouse or child, friend or country, involves a loss of freedom, a loss of autonomy, and, to some extent, a loss of self. In a prayer we read at every Jewish worship service, right before the *Sh'ma,* we say that God gave us commandments to guide our lives. A commandment both enslaves and liberates us at the same time; it frees yet entraps us. On the one hand, it gives us direction, provides bonding between us and God so that we need not stumble blindly through life—that is freedom. On the other hand, it tells us how to spend our time and money, what to eat and what not to eat, with whom we can associate, how to run our business, even how to speak appropriately to others—those are limitations. There is no aspect of life that is ignored by God's commandments.

Now this act of revelation, of giving commandments, we call, interestingly enough, *ahavat olam* or *ahavah rabah,* deep and abiding love. God loves us, so God limits our freedom, and God's freedom is limited as well. Every love relationship involves a certain loss of freedom. From now on, God is stuck with us, and we are bound to the Holy One. We can have no other gods, and

God cannot choose another people as representative. To be in love means to bind our soul to the soul of another. As Alan Bloom teaches, "It is becoming more human through our interconnectedness, a connection that transcends the isolation of personal selfishness, and in which the thought of oneself is inextricably bound up with the thought of the other." When we love, we must put the will of the other above our own.

The Talmud, that great compendium of Jewish law and lore, puts it this way: "When love is strong, a man and a woman can make their bed on the blade of a sword; but when love grows weak, sixty cubits is not large enough." In other words, when love is real, we are not so full of ourselves. We shrink in humility and make room for our lover. But when love is false, we are so preoccupied with ourselves that there is no room for anything but our desires, our needs, our selves—no room for our loved one— and no room, then, for love.

Compromise

I teach every couple that there are two types of compromise, and they have to decide which is appropriate for any given situation. The first is when one person wants X and the other wants Z so you decide to get Y. While neither partner got what he or she originally wanted in this type of compromise, no sides are chosen, no one feels like a loser.

A second type of compromise is when one partner gets to do X (with or without the other) and the other gets to do Z. In this scenario, each person gets what he or she really wanted in the first place. The challenge is to support one another, to feel good about the other person doing what he or she wants, or to at least not feel threatened by it. Of course, this type of compromise assumes that what the partners want is not toxic to the relationship itself. When partners are desirous of or are choosing behaviors that are unhealthy for the relationship, support at that point can be enabling, even destructive. We have to always make sure we are not being enablers, for there is no quicker way to destroy a relationship and the people in it.

Panim el Panim/*Communication*

A number of years ago, my wife, Karen, and I led a program for teens called the JFTY Urban Mitzvah Corps. During the day, these thirty-six high school students went out into the community to volunteer in a variety of settings—playgrounds, senior citizen centers, day care centers, Meals on Wheels—in an attempt to make the world a better place in which to live. In the evenings, we held programs to help them better understand the nature of our societal problems. And since we were all living together in a big house, we ended each night with a session designed to help build relationships and to deal with issues proactively, before they became problems. We called these sessions, *Panim el Panim* (pronounced pah-neem ehl pah-neem)/Face to Face.

The name comes from the Torah's description of Moses' communication with God. Moses, unlike previous prophets who saw God in dreams and visions, "spoke to God face to face, as a person speaks to a friend." Later, the Torah tells us that Moses "could not see God's face and live," so we understood *panim el panim* as a metaphor for how we want to communicate with others. While full disclosure remains our prerogative, *panim el panim* demands that what we choose to share be open and honest. To this day, I use the phrase *panim el panim* when I teach communication skills in workshops or in counseling sessions.

Panim el panim does not force us to share everything that is on our mind, every experience we have ever had, every thought, every fantasy. Some things, especially in close relationships, are best left as private matters or even secrets. We are entitled to have an inner life that is exclusively our own. Though what we share is our choice, how we share, if we want healthy relationships, must be accurate, clear, and honest. It must be shared out of concern for the other and the relationship itself. It must be shared with love. It must treat the other as an image of God in the world. In *panim el panim* communication, we must face our partner, physically or metaphorically, and say what it is we are thinking and feeling. Nothing short of that will do.

Whenever someone tells me they did not tell their true feelings because they were trying to protect the other, I let them know, as lovingly as I can, that I don't believe them. We rationalize our dishonesty all the time. But a lie is a lie. It will act like a little cancer, eating away at the fabric of the relationship, multiplying until there is nothing left. Of course, our disclosure will differ from person to person. How I tell my parents about why I quit my job will be different from how I tell my partner, and different from how I tell my children. I can be honest with all three still telling differing versions of the truth. But if *panim el panim* communication is my ideal, my goal, then truth it will be.

Helpful hint. We should always try to designate a time for *panim el panim* communication, either a regular part of our schedule or a specific request. Springing this kind of communication on others, especially if they are not used to it, can be overwhelming, even damaging. Doing this on the way to meet friends for an evening out, for example, is probably not a great idea. Also, before you choose to disclose anything, ask yourself the question "Does my partner really need to hear this?" If the answer is "No," hold on to it, perhaps share it with someone else, or let it go.

Fighting

I grew up in a household in which we fought openly, and loudly. Afterward, we were always quick to make up. My father, on the rare occasions when he struck us for some misbehavior, would soon after sit down, and with tears in his eyes, hug and kiss us.

If you (like my wife) did not grow up in a household in which the members fought with one another, then you probably think that fighting is a sign of unhealthy relationships. It is not. People who live together will inevitably have conflicts, usually caused by a difference of opinion about how something ought to be done. Fighting is one way of resolving conflicts. So long as the fight is fair, then it is okay to fight. Of course, if you can work out the conflict before it becomes a fight, so much the better.

Fighting fair ought to be a way for each person to discover and clarify his or her ideas and feelings, express them to the other, and seek a solution. It can also be a great emotional release of pent-up feelings. Fighting fair means we restrict ourselves to the issue(s) at hand. "Hitting below the belt" occurs when people dredge up the past, name-call, patronize, use sarcasm, mention other parties not germane to the fight, character-assassinate, or in any other way divert attention from the issue at hand. In a fair, healthy fight, partners will stay focused and make up when it is all over.

Most of us fight when we are angry, which is not too smart. Anger blinds us with its power and passion. It often prevents us from fighting fairly. If at all possible, I suggest waiting until your anger subsides before fighting. If you cannot, at least acknowledge the anger to your partner. It will help to contextualize all the inappropriate and hurtful things you will probably wind up saying.

Apartness

Just as we all have cycles in our lives, ups and downs, periods of great activity and accomplishment, down times, and plateaus, so do relationships. And every great relationship, whether it be between two partners, two friends, or an individual and God, will go through a period (or periods) that I call "the desert"—an extended time when nothing seems to be working and the partners feel like strangers. This is a time—days, weeks, or years after the honeymoon is over—when differences dominate, and we ask, "Who is this person?" In the Torah, this is represented by the Book of Numbers, in Hebrew, *BaMidbar*/In the Wilderness—a book that talks about the breakdown of the relationship between God and the generation freed from Egyptian slavery.

It is often during the desert period that friendships break up and partners consider divorce. When the relationship is between siblings or parents and children, it can be the time when contact is limited or even broken off. But it does not have to happen. If only we realize that there is not necessarily anything wrong with the relationship, that a period like this is as natural and normal as the falling-in-love stage, then we can accept this, hold on tight, talk about it, live through it, get some counseling help if we need it, and get to the other side.

Relationships that make it through the desert are stronger and healthier than those that do not. And even if the ultimate decision is to end the relationship, having made it through the desert will make us better partners in our next relationship.

Intimacy

While there may be hints of it earlier on, true intimacy is achieved in moments, often only after a lifetime of being present for one another. But it is just such moments that sustain us, that keep us going, that enable us to get through all the other stuff that is part and parcel of life itself. I see very few couples who have attained that level of closeness. But it is a thing of beauty when I do. They know and understand themselves. They know and accept each other. For if intimacy is about becoming one, then we must open up, trusting ourselves and our partners, and make way for the other to be him- or herself. Not what we want them to be, not what we expect them to be, just themselves—so that we can be ourselves.

My favorite metaphor for intimacy is a dance. On the dance floor, only couples who really know each other's moves, who do not hold on too tightly, who know when to create space between each other and when to embrace, only these couples are dancing, rather than merely moving. So it is with intimacy. We become one so that we may become ourselves.

The Book of Deuteronomy represents the intimacy achieved between God and the Jewish people. Moses looks back in honest and grateful reminiscence on the journey of forty years. While it was not always easy, while there were many moments that could have broken the relationship altogether, there the people stand, ready to enter the promised land. There is such a promised land waiting for every relationship. But it takes a lifetime of hard work and commitment to get there.

Sex

Though it may be easy for me to say this now, I am convinced that sexual relations belong exclusively in the context of a committed relationship. The notion that if we cannot be with the one we love we ought to love the one we are with treats sex as if it were nothing more than an exchange of bodily fluids. But sex is more than that. Or at least it can be. It is a type of intimacy that awakens us to our full humanity. It is our closest connection to the life force itself. It carries the potential for us to re-create ourselves, thereby making us God-like. And it is a physical enactment of the merger experience, the closest we may ever come to being one with the other. No wonder sex drives people crazy, unleashing all sorts of complex emotional and psychological baggage.

I realize that not every sexual encounter quite fulfills these expectations. Given the reality that most people wait until well into adulthood to partner or marry, the universal accessibility of birth control, and the acceptance of a wide variety of lifestyles, sex is and will remain for many people a pleasurable but primarily physical experience. I am neither naïve nor Pollyannaish enough to think that it might become otherwise. I accept the reality of the sexual mores of our time. Nevertheless, I think something has been lost in our sexual revolution and that it can be recaptured by committed partners who keep their sexual behavior exclusively between them.

Marriage

The word for marriage in Jewish tradition is *kiddushin* (pronounced k'doo-sheen). It comes from the root *koof, dalet, shin*, the letters used to form the word, "holy." The ideal notion of marriage in Judaism is "holiness." We partner to create holiness. When that holiness is present, we have a real marriage. When it is not, we may have a marriage on paper, but it is not a true marriage. This is succinctly stated in the rabbinic dictum "No man without a woman, no woman without a man, and neither the two of them without the presence of God." Every marriage is conceived of by Judaism as a ménage à trois. God is the third partner.

Now when I say "marriage" I am talking about that relationship of commitment that seeks to bring holiness between the partners and into the world. While the medieval rabbis could imagine this only in a heterosexual context, today, with our expanded understanding of human sexuality, we realize that the same *kiddushin* can also exist between partners of the same sex.

Kiddushin revolves around how we treat one another and the relationship we create, not the gender of the people creating it.

There is *kiddushin* in a marriage when each partner relates to the other as an image of God. When we communicate openly and honestly; when we nurture the other to his or her full human potential; when we compromise in a healthy manner; when there is room for us to grow; when we accept our differences without trying to change or co-opt the other; when we feel safe, committed, and secure; when there are appropriate boundaries; when the sexuality is intimate and pleasurable; when fighting is a battle over issues and ideas, not persons; when there is an ability to ask for and receive forgiveness; when doing for the other does not seem like a burden; when there is a mission that extends into the world and beyond the relationship itself; when there is laughter and joy—all of this helps to create *kiddushin* in a marriage. Such a marriage sustains its partners and delights all those with whom it comes in contact. While we may not sense *kiddushin* every minute of every day, still it remains our hope and our goal. A marriage that is not built on *kiddushin* is really no marriage at all.

Get

A *get* is literally a "Bill of Divorcement" issued by a rabbinic court for the purpose of dissolving a marriage. I include it here more generically in order to discuss how we might consider ending relationships in a holy way.

What do I mean by "holy"? Something God would approve of. We end a relationship in a holy way by giving thanks for all the good that came from it. We end a relationship in a holy way by blessing the other on his or her future journey without us. Letting go of any remaining anger, rancor, or bitterness will also clear a path for holiness to exist. Making sure, within the best of our ability, that each person has the financial wherewithal to go on with his or her life is also necessary. And finally, though not always possible, we create a holy ending by being available to the other through our ongoing support and love.

At a recent funeral, I noticed the ex-husband of the bereaved daughter of the deceased. I made it a point to go up to him later that day to tell him I thought it was great that he could be there. After all, this person had been his mother-in-law for many years. When relationships end, they do not have to be completely over. They can transform themselves into a new relationship that continues to have value and meaning in each person's life. When we end our relationships in a holy way, they can do just that.

Parenting

I can still remember with absolute clarity the moment I became a father. After some twenty-four hours of well-coached Lamaze breathing, hours of the most excruciating pain for which I could just "be there," holding Karen's hand, we were whisked off to the hospital delivery room, where I, surgically masked and hospital-gowned, was told to stand off to the side, waiting for the final moments of our baby's passage from womb to life. From that moment on it happened so quickly. Suddenly his head emerged. *Get the camera,* I remembered. *It's a boy's head, Ms. Sobel . . . looks like a boy.* Snap. *Yes, a boy . . .* Snap. They were holding him up. He looked so gray in the dim light. *Oh, my God, is he alive?* And then he gasped for breath, and I breathed; he cried with a sound that seemed more than physical and with tears in my eyes, I said the word *sh'heh'chee-ah-noo.* I did not manage more than that. *Sh'heh'chee-ah-noo.* The one word seemed enough, yet it paled in comparison to the experience. *Thank you, thank you, God, Creator of all Life, for having made me a father.* Those words that I finally managed to get out still echo in my ears more than seventeen years later, as that boy is turning into a beautiful young man.

To parent a child is to affirm life. It is to become responsible for the life that is placed in our care, to accept for a lifetime that which is given to us. It is the only human relationship that, once begun, can never be dissolved. To parent a child is to enter into a partnership with God, the ultimate parent.

Our children challenge us to look at the world all over again with the eyes of a first-time observer. For them, whether it is brushing their teeth or brushing yours, pointing to the light or pointing to your face in a photograph, all life is a wonder. And as we watch them discovering their world, we are given the opportunity to find the child within ourselves. Parenting is a confrontation with all our values. Our children force us to examine and reexamine all of our defenses and reasons, to hear the voices of our own parents and ask, "Is this what I really believe?" Parenting pushes us beyond what we thought were our limits to be nurturing, worrying, and self-sacrificing—to balance our needs with those of the child who needs us. To be a parent is to seek the spiritual in the mountains of daily mundane details, from diapers to car pools, which become the very stuff of our lives.

The decision to have a child is a totally personal one and is often beyond our control or power to influence. But for those who make that decision and are blessed to become parents, the experience allows us to be God-like, to become holy in imitation of God who is also holy. The Talmud teaches that parents are obligated to "enter their children into the covenant, to redeem them, to teach them Torah, to arrange a marriage, to teach them a craft, and some say, to teach them to swim." (The Talmud voices this in the masculine—fathers' obligations to their sons. I have contemporized it here to speak of parents and their children.) It is interesting to note that all these acts are also attributed to God and the Jewish people.

To teach Torah is to connect to the Holy through the holy

word. But what Torah will we teach? What messages will we give? When we began having children, Karen and I thought we had to be consistent, to know exactly what our beliefs were, what rituals we would incorporate, what practices we would observe, but we soon came to realize that the only Torah we could teach was the one that came from us and through us—that Torah which is ours to give.

God, we are told, gives Torah to Israel out of love for this people, and we are born, we become Israel on the day we receive it. The midrash compares God's gift of Torah to a mother nursing her child. Torah, like a mother's milk, is the sustaining substance of life, which comes from within us and is given freely to the child. I thought of that often as I watched Karen nurse our children. It was so natural, so perfect, so direct. Our children take Torah from us. We give it freely.

Growing up is a process of learning to be autonomous, free of our dependence on our parents. Our children, from the day they are born, are learning to live without us. And as we watch them gain mastery over their own world, from those first steps to the first time we turn over the car keys, there is a bittersweet tide that takes hold of us. We applaud—they are healthy and normal; we fight back the tears—these days flee so quickly. To teach a trade and find a spouse was the ancients' way of telling us we had to raise our children to leave us and make their own way in the world.

Raising children, we are told, is a matter of pushing them away with the left hand and bringing them closer with the right. Parenting means learning to let go. The kabbalah teaches us that originally God filled the entire universe, but because God so loved us, there was this voluntary process of contraction (*tzim tzum*) to make room for us. As parents, we too have to learn to contract ourselves to give our children the space to learn and grow up, to become the people God means for them to be.

But we cannot just love our children. Love is not enough.

We concretize our relationship through acts, both big and small. Two big acts are to circumcise and redeem. We circumcise to enter our children into the covenant with God; we redeem to let our children know we want them to be a part of our lives. The English word "parent" comes from the Latin "to give birth to." In Hebrew, the word for parent is *horah* (pronounced *hoe-rah*), to enlighten or to raise. The one who raises a child is the child's true parent.

And some say to teach them to swim. My friend and teacher Rabbi Bill Cutter suggested that swimming is a metaphor for teaching our children to deal with all types of emergency situations. The urge to protect our children seems to be the most natural one of all. Like the mother eagle, which flies with her young on her back, we want to put ourselves between our children and danger or harm. We do that instinctively. But when our children are injured or, God forbid, killed, we realize that our powers are limited. Perhaps the best we can do is teach them to be careful, to protect themselves.

In the dangerous world in which we live, such a suggestion is fraught with implications. Do we give our children martial arts lessons, or teach them to mind their own business? Are they to be kind and hospitable, or wary of strangers? We are not eagles, and even if we were, there would still come a time when our young would have to fly by themselves. We will teach them, and worry, and pray.

When Ari was a toddler, we took him to swimming lessons at our synagogue's pool. I never knew that doing a mitzvah, fulfilling a commandment, could be so much fun. As I watched him paddling around the pool, laughing and splashing, I thought to myself, At least this is one source of danger we can do something about.

The rabbis taught us that to become a parent is to lose one's peace of mind. I have found that to be so very true. On the other hand, what I once put down as vicarious living—*q'velling* (pronouced k'vell-ing) from our children's successes—I now find to be a genuine pleasure in my life. In fact, I can think of nothing that gives me greater satisfaction and joy. Though it may cost us our peace of mind, by parenting a child we also gain the potential to transcend ourselves. We lose our isolation, our aloneness, our temporality, and through our connection to our children we become bound up in all of life.

Parenting Our (Aging) Parents

There are two ways of understanding time. One is linear, in which there are beginnings, middles, and ends. This is our notion of history. Another way of looking at time, though, is as a cycle. There, time is repeated; every beginning is also an ending, for time never really ceases. We can look at our lives either way. There is a Terry Bookman who was born, who is living, and who someday will die. Or, there is a Terry Bookman who came into being, who continues to be, and who will exist forever, for what we call death is simply the body's release of its eternal soul. What is eternal can never really die.

In linear time, aging is a negative—the breaking down of the body on its way to its ultimate demise. Aging is about limitation, and so no one wants to get old, unable to do the things that she or he used to do, becoming a burden on others. But in cyclical time, aging is merely the return to the beginning. We begin as helpless babies, totally dependent on others for our every need. Most everyone loves babies, and most people are only too happy to tend to them. Aging and becoming ill is, in this manner of thinking, about dependence, about becoming a baby once again. It becomes our responsibility, if we are fortunate, to parent those who parented us. It means they have lived long enough to return to the beginning.

Of course, all of this is fraught with difficulty. Our parents may not be so easy to be around in this process. Though needy and increasingly dependent on us, they may not be all that willing to have us serve in that role. They may be in denial that they need the help, or angry and frustrated because they do. We may view such increased responsibility, especially as we have our own busy lives to live, as a burden. We may resent them, fear their death, or just be overwhelmed by the prospect. If the world of an infant is all ego, all "I," then this cyclical return of our parents might explain why they become so self-focused, and self-absorbed, telling the same stories about themselves over and over again. It is not easy. Our parents may not be all that likable.

Nevertheless, parenting our aging parents is an incredible opportunity to return to them some of the love and nurture they gave to us so freely. It is a fleeting chance to see ourselves as we may yet come to be. And for those who have children, it is the best role modeling we could ever hope to provide. My great-grandfather, my *zeyde*, died in his daughter's (my grandmother's) home. Though I was only nine years old at the time, I will never forget the love and respect she showed him and how she felt it a privilege to take care of him in that way. Every family that I have ever seen extend itself to do this for a parent has felt blessed by the experience. Though I pray that for us it will be many years away, I hope Karen and I will be able to do this for our own parents when the time comes. This will require the willingness of both of them and a great deal of planning—appropriate physical space, the cooperation of other family members, a medical insurance program that allows it, qualified health caretakers, flexibility in our own schedules, lots of time and patience. I know that having them close to us as they begin the breakdown process is both difficult and rewarding. Just the way it is supposed to be.

Friendship

Most men I know complain that they do not have good friends like they used to when they were growing up or just getting started in their adult lives. I think this is true. As men begin to focus on career and family, the relationship most likely to get pushed aside is friendship. What a loss that is.

I believe that what is most profound about friendship is the opportunity it provides us for nonsexual, yet genuine intimacy. For all its wonder, sex also complicates relationships. It unavoidably brings with it issues of power, attraction, boundaries, and control. No matter who the partners are, sex is almost always tinged with insecurity, uncertainty, and fear. With friends, we can simply be ourselves, know that we are accepted, and share our deepest secrets, the innermost places of our hearts. Though we love our friends and they love us, in a way there is less at stake in friendship, and so we can be even more of ourselves.

Friendship also provides us with other outlets to meet some of our needs. In our own time, with the breakdown of the extended family and the great mobility that we experience, when partners and families are asked to become the center of our world, having good friends can take some of the pressure off those primary relationships. Friends become extensions of our hearts, and those that remain through the test of time are a source of blessing in our lives.

Nature

Not all significant relationships are with people. God's creation extends to the natural world and to its animals. And in truth, many of us have an easier time connecting to God by being outdoors, sailing on the ocean, skiing down a mountain, watching a sunset, or caring for and playing with our pets and animals. I used to love watching a friend of mine, Beverly Shapson (may her memory be a blessing), walking through her all-natural garden. Each plant, every leaf, held meaning and power for her. There were stories and magic everywhere. She would pass my window every morning, walking with her dog, Sunshine—never on a leash, the two of them were of one mind. When she died, her dog fell rapidly into decline and passed away soon after. I am convinced it was from a broken heart.

The Jewish tradition does not allow us to say *kaddish* (the prayer of mourning) for a pet. But the fact that the question was asked, and is asked, convinces me that the love we can have for an animal entrusted into our care is genuine and real. I know I see it in my boys and their caring for our dog, Jed. And I have seen the real sense of loss in others when their pets die. Animals are an extension of ourselves. Perhaps they represent our innocence, or our ability to nurture and care for another without any ulterior motive. In their capacity to be always present and in the moment, perhaps they give us a model for how we would like to be in the world. Wordlessly, they and the world around us, communicate to us of the One, and show us that all is one.

Getting Started

In a way, we already are. Each of us is in relationship with someone or another. Literally, we do not need to begin.

But perhaps you want to raise up the quality of those relationships, bringing more of yourself to them and getting more from them. Perhaps you do not like the way a certain relationship is playing itself out in your life and want to correct or improve it. Or perhaps there is someone with whom you are not yet in relationship and would like to be.

Even if we do not have a willing partner, we can make some

unilateral decisions about how we want to be in relationship with others. Of course, ultimately, relationships require all the interested partners to work together toward the same end. But in the meantime, I can alter my behavior, my responses, my language, all of which will, in and of itself, change the relationship. Sometimes such change is not welcome. People get used to unhealthy interactions and, consciously or not, go to great lengths to keep the status quo. Many times I have seen the change agent be vilified for changing the rules. A woman who insists on an egalitarian relationship after years of "being taken care of" by her husband will often be met with resistance. That husband may feel threatened or useless in the new role of equal. Grown children who insist on an adult-to-adult relationship with their parents may find their parents unwilling or incapable of such alteration after a lifetime of being mom or dad.

Nevertheless, even if we cannot stop the merry-go-round of unhealthy or dysfunctional relationships, we can, ourselves, get off and refuse to participate any longer. If we are in a relationship in which we feel unloved, then we can become more loving ourselves. It is amazing how much more love we feel when we act lovingly toward another. Often individuals go outside the relationship to give and find that love. While this may feel like a solution to the problem, it is only a temporary salve, and will generally create more problems that it hopes to solve. If we are unhappy with the way our communication is going in a particular relationship, getting help with the messages we are sending and changing them can have a dramatically positive effect. While the old adage "It takes two to tango" still holds true, in terms of getting started with healthy relationships, one person's effort can often be the catalyst to good things. And even if it does not accomplish that in one particular relationship, the lessons learned can be applied to all others.

Just a word about Shabbat. Though the Sabbath day is about many things, one way of looking at it is as a gift of time for focusing on interpersonal relations. On Shabbat, time stands still. We shut off the outside world of obligations and interference and simply allow ourselves to be with one another. No phone, no television, no beepers, no stores—just you, your partner, family, friends, and community. Shabbat can be a fully relational day to help you catch up and be with one another, heal the wounds caused by a week of running around and seeing but not really being with one another. A time for relaxed meals instead of quick bites on the run, real conversations instead of sound bites of informational exchange, quality *and* quantity time instead of ships passing in the night. Shabbat can be a transformational tool for strengthening and renewing our relationships, both near and far. If you have not already incorporated the Sabbath day into your week, it is waiting for you to discover. So are all the people you love and who love you.

About the Author

Rabbi Terry Bookman is Senior Rabbi at Temple Beth Am, the largest congregation in Miami, Florida. Widely published in religious journals, he is active in dozens of Jewish, spiritual, and rabbinic associations. Rabbi Bookman frequently lectures to community groups and religious leaders of all faiths, and has launched an on-line spiritual forum at *www.betham-miami.org* through which he offers spiritual guidance to hundreds of participants each day. He has written and produced CDs, tapes, and music to enhance daily spirituality. He is also the author of *The Busy Soul*.